CROTCHETS
A FEW SHORT MUSICAL NOTES
BY PERCY A. SCHOLES

Essay Index Reprint Series

BOOKS FOR LIBRARIES PRESS
FREEPORT, NEW YORK

42650

First Published 1924
First Reprinting in this Series 1966
Second Reprinting 1969

STANDARD BOOK NUMBER:
8369-0855-4

LIBRARY OF CONGRESS CATALOG CARD NUMBER:
67-22115

PRINTED IN THE UNITED STATES OF AMERICA

CROTCHETS

CONTENTS

		PAGE
CONCERTS AND AUDIENCES :		
I	WHAT DOES THE AUDIENCE HEAR ?	3
II	A PLEA FOR ALL-ROUND ART	8
III	ANNOTATED PROGRAMMES	13
IV	A HOLIDAY TASK	18
V	OUR PAUPER PUBLIC	24
VI	THE ETHICS OF APPLAUSE	28
WHAT THE PUBLIC WANTS :		
I	BEASTLY TUNES	34
II	THE POPULAR PROGRAMME	40
"FOR THE GOOD OF MUSIC"		45
THE PRESENT-DAY PROBLEM		50
WELSH SINGERS AND ENGLISH CRITICS		58
A FEW SUGGESTIONS UPON POPULAR MUSIC :		
I	" DOPE "	66
II	SOME " SERIOUS CRITICISM "	71
III	MORE " SERIOUS CRITICISM "	78
IV	QUALITY IN MUSIC	82
A FEW REMARKS ON OPERA :		
I	THE PACE OF OPERA	87
II	OPERATIC IMPROBABILITIES	91
III	OPERA AS SEEN BY AN ACTOR	96
IV	DEBUSSY AND " DASH "	100
A HAUNTED HEAD		105
THE MUSIC OR THE MAKING ?		
I	SILK PURSES AND SOW'S EARS	110
II	SOMETHING FROM NOTHING	114
WHAT IS MELODY ?		119
SOME NOTES ON SCRIABIN :		
I	SCRIABIN AS STUDENT	125
II	SCRIABIN'S PROCESSES OF COMPOSITION	128
III	SCRIABIN AND " LAW "	132
IV	SCRIABIN AS PIANIST	137
V	SCRIABIN AS THINKER	141

PAGE

SOME VIEWS ON STRAVINSKY:
I THE "RITE" AND THE WRONG OF IT . 144
II HONEST DOUBT 151
III STRAVINSKY IN THE NURSERY . . . 157

POLYTONALITY AND ATONALITY:
I POLYTONALITY 162
II ATONALITY 167

COLOUR AND SOUND 173

THE MIND MADE UP 178

HANDEL AND BACH:
I HANDEL AND THE HORSE'S LEG . . . 183
II HANDEL AND BACH AS WE HEAR THEM TO-DAY 188

SHAKESPEARE'S MUSIC: A THEORY 194

WORDS AND MUSIC:
I WE WANT THE WORDS 202
II "A CONCERTO ON THE LARYNX" . . 206

CHORAL SOCIETY PROBLEMS 211

KREISLERIANA:
I THE FIDDLER'S REPERTORY . . . 223
II "CHACONNE À SON GOUT" 228

THE PROMISE OF THE PAST 233

YOUTH AND MUSIC:
I BACK TO SCHOOL 239
II THE CHILD AND THE GRAMOPHONE . . 243
III "AN UNMITIGATED CURSE" . . . 247

IMPERSONAL TRUTH IN CRITICISM 252

SHALL WE RECONSIDER WOLF? 257

SANTLEY 262

CHURCH MUSIC:
I WHAT THE ORGANIST SAID 267
II CHURCH MUSIC ABROAD 272

THE O.B. AND MUSIC 282

"RE YOUR LETTER TO HAND". 287

CROTCHETS

CROTCHETS

CONCERTS AND AUDIENCES

I. What does the Audience hear?

WHAT does the audience hear? I mean the normal everyday type of audience—the sort of audience you get at a Queen's Hall Symphony or London Symphony orchestral performance. And in asking the question I am not thinking of those occasions when we go out of our way to baffle the plain man with "Rites of Spring" and "Colour Symphonies" and "Planets," and pieces in which the musical idiom is (in places, at any rate) sufficiently novel to justify a little honest bewilderment at a first hearing, but of the simple classics—Beethoven symphonies, and the like. Take the Fifth Symphony, for instance; in such a piece as this—What does the audience hear?

I am prompted to ask this question by one or two recent disasters. At a Three Choirs Festival the Franck symphony was played. I was not present, but I believe this piece was the last upon the programme and that the conclusion of the first movement was taken by the cleric in charge for the conclusion of the whole piece, whereupon he pronounced the Benediction and discharged the congregation. We will

3

not base too much on this incident ; a movement of
a sonata or symphony has a completeness in itself, and
we can, perhaps, blame the person in question with
nothing worse than a non-acquaintance with Franck
and a too vague knowledge of the general habits of
symphonies. What looks like a worse case was
reported lately by the " Pall Mall Gazette " :

" Last Sunday week at the Temple Church there
was a dramatic pause in the anthem. No doubt
the composer thought he had wrought well in working
up to a climax, followed by a brief silence. But the
silence was not too brief for Dean Inge to rush in
where an angel might have hesitated. He started
the bidding prayer and the silent choir—remained
silent."

But here again we can afford to be charitable. At
all events we should need to know what the anthem
was, and where the disaster occurred, before we pronounced judgment on the Dean ; it may be that the
trap was such as we might any of us fall into. In
any case the Dean is reputed frankly to describe
himself as the most unmusical of men and we have
no more right to taunt him with a slip of this kind
than he would have to chaff us in his light and playful
way about an ignorant remark on the subject of,
say, Eugenics.

A much worse case is that reported (by " R. C." in
the " Daily Mail ") of Cortot's last recital :

" The enthusiasts who drowned the last bars of
Op. 25, Nos. i and ii, will do well to glance at the
printed page before they next go to a Chopin recital.

Strange that, after hundreds and thousands of performances of the great A minor study, there are still
people who will not wait to listen to the upward-
rushing scales of the last bar."

This is a different case altogether. Those people
came to the Wigmore Hall expressly to hear music,
and yet, if " R. C." is to be believed, they could not
have passed the simplest examination in the art of
listening. All this happened a few days after I had
been publicly hinting at " grave doubts as to the
musicality of a Pachmann audience "; it confirms
my doubts (but widens them, so that they now apply
to piano recital audiences in general), and leads me
to recount the circumstance which first made me a
serious doubter. What follows relates to a Pachmann
recital of four or five years back at which I was present. I took particular note of the occurrence, and
the facts as I relate them can be relied upon.

The case is one of a complete non-understanding of
one of the most strikingly effective passages in one
of the very best-known piano pieces—the break before
the end of Chopin's Nocturne in G, Op. 37, No. 2.
Professional musicians and keen amateur pianists
must pardon me if I spend a few lines of space on a
description of the nocturne and a few bars of it in
music type ; I am constantly made aware by letters
I receive that I have amongst my readers not merely
educated musicians, but also a good many people
with little technical knowledge of music, and as I
feel that musical criticism and discussion are generally
read by too restricted a class, I value this double
suffrage and wish to retain it. The piece of which I

am speaking has two main themes, each of them the very perfection of poetic beauty ; they contrast with one another in style and in content, the second one being more melodic in style and deeper in mood. Their arrangement in relation to one another is simple ; it can be expressed in the formula A-B-A-B-A. But on its last appearance the first theme (" A ") is broken off unexpectedly and dramatically. A pause follows, and then, most imaginatively, the composer ends in his deeper mood with a brief reference to " B." The whole appreciation of the piece depends on a recognition (conscious or sub-conscious) of its beautifully managed alternations of themes, and consequently of mood. One would be tempted to say that if an audience could not recognize and recall these it was quite incapable of appreciation of musical beauty. Moreover, the dramatic pause takes its whole force from the fact that the passage which precedes it is palpably incomplete, its last chord being a discord— a chord of transition, not a chord of rest. It is as if the composer were about to end in his more cheerful mood when, in a flash, a thought passes through his mind which brings back his more solemn (almost sorrowful) mood, and on this he ends. It is a simple touch of pure genius—a real " inspiration."

Will it be believed that on the occasion of which I speak an audience which had appeared spellbound by the beauty of one of Chopin's most poetic pieces, perfectly interpreted, took the mere cessation of sound to mean the completion of the piece, and broke in with frantic applause ? This was not the sin of a mere two or three tone-deaf, or stone-deaf, people

who happened to notice that the pianist had taken his hands from the keyboard ; it was the act of probably fully one-half of those present. The conclusion must be that an audience of this type cannot readily follow the construction of a piece of music (and music of both the " classical " and " romantic " periods, however imaginative, admittedly depends for effect largely on conscious or sub-conscious perception of its main lines and details of construction), and, especially, that it has no appreciative perception whatever of harmonic values. Most musicians would agree, I think, in regarding as hopeless the individual who could take the rapidly modulating passage shown in the first three bars of the extract I have given as prophetic of an immediate conclusion, and could, moreover, take the " interrupted cadence " as a final cadence and the " diminished seventh " chord at the beginning of the fourth bar as the final chord of the piece. The revelation that our piano recital audiences are largely made up of such people is, I think, startling.

II. A Plea for All-round Art

A short time ago nine young architects were shut each in his narrow cell for thirty-six hours to make what they call their " esquisses," upon the subsequent working out of which, during the ten weeks to follow, an award was to be made entitling the winner to three years' residence at the British School at Rome. Compassion prompted me to try to give one of these prospective prisoners a last flickering gleam of pleasure before his dark days of trial began, and I took him to a Gerhardt recital at the Queen's Hall. No sooner were we seated, however, than he gave a quick glance round, shuddered, and to my sympathetic and alarmed inquiring look could only gasp " The Architecture ! Why are concert rooms always so horrible ? " For the honour of music I felt compelled to remind my young friend in a whisper that the music room had been designed not by a musician, but by—an architect. But with him I deplore the ugliness of our London concert halls.

The general point emerging from this complaint is our willingness, when occupied in producing art in one branch, unthinkingly to sacrifice all the other branches. Take further examples from this same occasion. The front cover of the programme in its fourteen or fifteen lines of type employed seven or eight different "founts," and eight or nine different sizes, and it had a crude block at the top designed to advertise the concert agent, and another at the bottom designed to advertise the maker of the piano. It was no worse than nine out of ten of the programmes we critics see daily, yet from a typographical point of view it was a horror—a mere mess of ugly blue lettering, dispersed higgledy-piggledy over a large surface of shiny, unpleasant paper. The back of the programme carried an announcement of the next recital, displayed in exactly the same inartistic way. The interior pages gave the German and English words of the songs in parallel columns, and, at first, startled you with the suggestion that the former language is much more concise than the latter, since in some cases the translation of the poems took double the space of the original, but you looked again and found that this alarming distension was due to maltreatment by the compiler. I give one verse as an example :

THE GERMAN

Einst, o Wunder! entblüht, auf meinem Grabe,
Eine Blume der Asche meines Herzens ;
Deutlich schimmert auf jedem Purpurblättchen :
Adelaïde !

THE ENGLISH

Soon, oh wonder, oh wonder, upon my tomb will
   blossom,
Oh wonder, upon my tomb will blossom,
One small flower from my heart's ashes springing, my
   fond heart's ashes springing,
On its petals, on its petals one name will brightly
   glisten, one name will brightly glisten.
Can you not guess it ? Can you not guess it ?
Soon, oh wonder, soon oh wonder, yes, soon on my
   tomb a flower will blossom,
One small flower from my fond heart's ashes springing,
   this fond heart's ashes springing,
On its petals, on its petals one name will brightly
   glisten.
Adelaide only ! Adelaide only ! brightly, brightly,
One name will brightly glisten, one name will brightly
   glisten :
Adelaide only ! Adelaide only ! Adelaide only !

Could there be any worse example of the neglect of
all other arts by the musician and his agent than

such a perversion of the poet's lines as this and the fact that throughout this book of words of fifteen songs the poet was only in two cases mentioned ? It is the poets (or people thinking themselves to be such) who supply the whole material of thought and word for the composer's musical treatment, yet, their handiwork having been distorted in the process of setting, their very names are given over to oblivion. Only the music matters !

Can I safely say a word about another inartistic practice—the custom of advertising pianos upon the platform ? Here is this great artist Gerhardt, like every artist, great and small, compelled by the commercial customs of the day to take her stand before us beside a line of brutal poster-type lettering announcing the maker of the instrument that accompanies her. So far has complaisance in this matter gone that when Strauss was here a few weeks earlier, a piano was placed behind him apparently merely for the advertisement of its makers, since the programme contained no piece of piano music, the songs were all orchestrally accompanied, and not a note of the instrument was or could have been heard the whole evening.

I have spoken above of the outrage to the poet of overlooking his very existence. What about the outrage to him and the composer of making the dramatic words of the one and setting of the other a mere medium for the display of the subtle and wonderful art of Lieder-singing ? Surely this can be charged when a man's song, such as Beethoven's " Adelaïde " or his " Mailied," is sung by a woman, however accomplished. Is there no inartistic absurdity in a woman

publicly declaiming, as Gerhardt did on the occasion
in question, such lines as those just quoted, or these
which follow :

> O, maiden, maiden, I love thee well,
> That thou lov'st me thy soft glances tell.

You are probably so accustomed to this solecism (com-
mitted daily by the most eminent women vocalists)
that you are astonished I should be unwilling to
tolerate it. Then let me put upon the platform of
the Queen's Hall Mr. John Coates, and compel him
against his will and at the point of the revolver (for
no lesser persuasion would avail with any self-respect-
ing male performer) coyly to sing another song of
Beethoven's :

> O would I were wed to thee,
> My life with thine enlinking !
> A maiden's speech reserved must be,
> Whate'er she may be thinking.
> But yet no bashful blushes steal,
> As I warm-hearted kisses feel.

It is curious that convention should allow to the one
sex what it would not for one moment allow to the
other. Here, then, is sauce for the goose that is not
such for the gander.

Small points all these, you say ! So they seem, yet
consideration of them takes us right down to this
bedrock question of principle—whether a musician is
a mere specialist in music or whether he is not rather
an Artist—whose particular medium of expression
happens to be that of tone. But I do not wish to

be unfair, and perhaps should remind you that the practitioners of other arts than music are also one-sided. I have observed sometimes in the Press announcements of the Annual Chelsea Arts Ball a programme of music to be performed that could only be sufficiently avenged were we musicians to invite Chelsea to an evening entertainment and treat it to a coloured crayon display by a one-eyed pavement artist.

Note.—A few days after this article appeared Gerhardt gave another recital, and it was pleasant to find the printing and editing of the programme greatly improved. The other evils remain. They are, of course, just as common with other singers as with her, and what has been said above is not intended to have any narrowly personal application.

III. ANNOTATED PROGRAMMES

There is no greater sham amongst our many concert-room shams than that of the annotated programme. It is prepared in a style that implies its careful perusal and then thrust into our hands as we enter the concert room and hear the orchestra tuning. We begin to devour our shillingsworth—when at once the cursed music starts, making reading impossible. It is like the trick that used at some continental stations to be played on hungry travellers, who were induced, on the strength of an announced stop for lunch or dinner, to get out, go to the buffet and pay a *prix fixe* for the excellent meal detailed on the menu, and then, nicely settled to its consumption, recalled hastily by the whistle to a train already in motion before they had time adequately to express their views to the head-waiter or the station-master. " Enter Ariel, like a harpy ; claps his wings upon the table ; and with a quaint device the banquet vanishes "—this very same old game, but reversed, Alonzo, Sebastian, and Antonio being whisked from the table instead of the table from them.

The introduction of the annotated programme is, I think, usually credited to Professor Ella, who used the device in connection with his Musical Union Concerts in 1845. But I have lately noted that the erudite critic of the " Yorkshire Post," Mr. Herbert Thompson, traces the idea back so far as one Knecht (turn him up in Grove), who ran orchestral concerts at Biberach, in Swabia, long ago, in 1790. I note from the books of reference that Knecht was for some time Professor of Literature at Biberach, but later turned orchestral conductor. The combination of talents and interests certainly seems one that was likely to produce a literary-musical contrivance such as the annotated programme, so probably Knecht actually was the inventor. Then, too, slightly before Ella, John Thomson, Professor of Music at Edinburgh University, seems to have done something similar in connection with the Reid concerts there, of which he was, I think, the first director. Grove says : " The book of words contained analytical remarks by him on the principal pieces—probably the first instance of such a thing," but as regards the last part of this remark, if Mr. Thompson on Mr. Thomson is right, Grove on pro-grammes is wrong. Now if Knecht and Thomson were sensible men they supplied the programmes before the

concert-day ; Ella certainly did so. It was not his
intention either to set people reading when they should
be listening or listening when they should be reading.

Taking into consideration the needs of his period,
nobody has ever written better annotated programmes
than Sir George Grove himself. His idea as to their
aims was thus stated :

The fact that a movement is written on a definite
plan or " form," and governed by rules more or less
rigid, though obvious to the technical musician, is
news to many an amateur ; and yet without understanding such facts it is impossible fully to appreciate
the intention or the power of the composer. In
following the scheme of the music, the hearer adds
to the pleasure of the sounds the pleasure of the
intellect. In addition to this there are few great
pieces of music about which historical or biographical
facts as to the origin and progress of the work, etc.,
connecting the music with the personality of the
composer, may not be stated so as to add materially
to the pleasure and profit of the hearer.

If you want to see how Grove carried out that aim
get his " Beethoven and his Nine Symphonies "
(Novello), which is merely an expansion of the
annotated programmes he wrote for performances of
the symphonies at the Crystal Palace. Were the
Crystal Palace programmes sold in advance ? I am
too young a London concert-goer to say, but I have
a huge collection of the programmes, picked up from
time to time, and so have many musicians, British
and foreign. They are still regularly quoted in the

catalogues of second-hand booksellers, and are, indeed, a good deal sought after.

If annotated programmes were needed in Grove's day, still more are they needed now, when so many composers of so many styles and idioms are composing music with so many different aims, avowed or implied. The most useful feature of the account given of any new work in (say) the programmes of Mr. Kalisch at the " Phil " is often the music-type examples of the main themes. But to sit with the programme before one's eyes, watching anxiously for the appearance of a " second subject introduced by the oboe, with accompaniment of strings and harp, soft flute shake and chords on the horns " is detective work unsuited to any hearer who has come to enjoy *music*. What the keen man ought to do is to get those themes well into his head at home (probably with the aid of the piano). There is no better preparation for the hearing of a new work than a foreknowledge of the " themes," since, knowing these, the sense of strangeness during actual performance vanishes, and one is merely watching with interest the behaviour of old friends. I know at present only one or two concert organizations that send their clients the programmes in advance. These are the Leeds Choral Union, another big North Country society, I think, at Liverpool, and a concert society in some smaller place in Scotland. I am sorry to give such vague references, but I am preparing this for press hundreds of miles from my files upon which are preserved the letters which reached me when I first broached this subject in the Press. I feel sure, however, that I am right in saying that there is no

London musical society, or concert organization of any
kind, that issues its annotated programmes before the
concert day.

How can we all have our programmes in advance?
First cut down the cost, and then issue the programme
(as the merest matter of common sense) *with the tickets.*
When the audience gathers for the next London
Symphony Orchestra concert it will be asked to pay
the usual shilling for the usual lavishly-got-up thirty-
eight-page compilation of two pages of title, one of
list of directors, solicitors, bankers, and auditors, one
of list of the orchestra itself, one of its forthcoming
provincial engagements, six of its coming London
concerts, five of catalogue of the orchestra's library,
five of advertisements, one of the evening's programme
in brief, and (at last I come to them!) sixteen of
detailed description of the pieces in the programme.
A great many people will refuse the thing at the price,
and those who buy it will not have time to read it,
especially as where they have come in groups of two,
three and four, only one shilling will be spent by the
whole group. This system is no speciality of the
L.S.O. Every orchestral concert scheme follows it.
When we get a real business man in charge of orchestral
concerts he will cut out all superfluous pages in the
programme, print it neatly but cheaply, without an
expensive cover, add 3*d.* to the price of the ticket,
supply it in advance gratis to all when they buy
their tickets, and perhaps even send it post-free to
applicants, as useful " publicity." He will include
advertisements, but will get better prices for them,
on the grounds of the bigger circulation and the greater

leisure of the reader. Moreover, his programmes will be seen in tubes and 'buses, and on the tables of subscribers for some days before each concert, and will certainly tend to increase his audiences.

IV. A HOLIDAY TASK

How would you like your young Adolphus to come home with a task of this sort?

Write down during the holidays what the following are : According to Cocker, Turbine, Confidence Trick, Rotten Borough, Bail, Blizzard, Simnel Cake, Mausoleum, En Garçon, Peter's Pence, Sixpenny, Googly, Taking Silk, Cenotaph, King's Evil, Simony, Suffragan Bishop, Rotation of Crops, Stygian Darkness, O.P. side, a Milled Coin, the Heel of Achilles, La Belle Sauvage, Sweated Labour, Conduct Money, Normal Temperature, Watered Capital, Index Finger, Packed Meeting, Solar Plexus, the Curse of Scotland, Opposite Number, the Vulgate, Temple Bar, Blacklead, the Dunmow Flitch, Blue John, Stalagmite, Boycott, Eight Bells, Coral, Stipendiary Magistrate, Chokedamp, Trinity House, Morris Tube, Bencher, Pidgin-English, Blazed Trail, Boxing Day, Spate, Starting Gate, Suffolk Punch, Regelation, a Tontine Policy, the Lake Poets, Lych Gate, Sinecure, Poet Laureate, Marseillaise, Hall Mark, Privilege of Parliament, Queensberry Rules, Breeches-buoy, Britannia Metal, Conscience Money, Tynwald Hill, Round Robin, Topsawyer, Utopian, a Man of Straw, Grotta del Cane, Job's Comforter, Terrier, Vinegar Bible, Santa Claus, the King over the Water, Rubric, Moonrakers, Hunting a Bagman, A Sop to Cerberus.

The headmaster who set that calls it a " Christmas

Holiday Employment for the Boys," but you and I know well that it will turn out to be one for the parents. " Dad, what's ' Regelation,' and what does ' Hunting a Bagman ' mean ? " And then poor Dad's reputation for omniscience will be gone ! So on behalf of Dad I am going to point out to the Rev. ——, of —— School, that the list he has compiled (and sent in triumph to last Wednesday's " Times ") is very defective, in that it omits any reference to the very subject upon which the public is most ignorant ; and to give him, in his turn, a " Christmas Holiday Employment," a perfectly reasonable one (one which as a civilized man, attending concerts like a Christian, he should have no difficulty in disposing of in a few of his spare moments), we will compile him a little list of terms such as every intelligent listener needs to understand if he is to read with any profit his " Annotated Programme."

We will not laboriously search any Musical Dictionary for the terms ; each of them shall be one which has actually been put before a London concert audience. Here, then, is our Head's Holiday Task :

Write down during the holidays an explanation of the following : Acciaccatura, Duple Time, Solo Organ, Con alcuna licenza, Enharmonic Modulation, Passepied, Appoggiatura, Exposition, Phantasy, Cyclic Forms, Phrase, Reed Pipes, Augmentation, Fugato, Programme Music, Glockenspiel, Ripieno, Cadenza, Ground Bass, Rosalia, Oboe da Caccia, Cavatina, Half-Close, Saltarello, Chalumeau, Harpsichord, Saxhorn, Affrettato, Double Counterpoint, Passacaglia, Allemande, Pentatonic Scale, Cor Anglais, Modes,

Figured Bass, Aubade, Fioriture, Pizzicato, Basset Horn, Glissando, Quarter-Tone, Cachucha, Ritornel, Canon, Stretto, Gruppetto, Rubato, Corno di Bassetto, Motto Theme, Chaconne, Harmonics, Sarrusophone, Oboe d'Amore, Counter-subject, Whole-Tone-Scale, Loure, Contrafagotto, Leading-Note, Viol da Gamba, Chamber Music, Heckelphone, Serpent, Inversion, Ciacona, Saxophone, Idée Fixe, Sextolet, Ländler, Compound Time, Invertible Counterpoint, Sordino, Concertino, Concertstück, Tonic, Leitmotif, Les Cinq, Les Six.

After looking through that little list (which might easily have been longer, but which in fairness I have restricted to about the same length as the one which prompted it), perhaps you will realize what the plain man feels like when, having been tempted to visit the Queen's Hall, and having paid his hard-earned five shillings at the door, he hands over still another in exchange for a document which he finds to be written in a foreign language. I do not believe musicians realize the position of that plain man, or they would be a little kinder to him when they write about their art.

I begin to feel that the terminology of music is really rather wicked. If you yourself can do the holiday task I have set (do it correctly, at a sitting, without books of reference), I venture to say that you are either a well-trained professional musician or else a keen amateur who has made music his hobby for a good many years. To you the mystic word " Op." has no remaining terrors : you can distinguish readily between " figured bass," " double bass," and " ground bass " ; you know (what I have found by experience hundreds of educated people do not know) the difference of function between organ pedals, piano pedals, harp pedals, and harmonium pedals, and do not confuse any one of those functions with anything connected with the playing of a " pedal clarinet," when you read of this latter in a programme reference to (say) Vincent d'Indy's " Fervaal." Then I suppose there is no lurking muddle in your mind as to saxhorn and saxophone; " double counterpoint " has a definite meaning to you and does not suggest vaguely an extra blanket in winter; and you could smile, as I did, at an examination paper I had to mark the other day, in which a well-known hymn tune of Tallis was described : " The tenor sings the same tune as the treble, but four notes after it all the way ; such pieces are called Deans." And you would take the writer's humorous meaning in another paper I saw a few weeks ago, in which fugal stretto was described as " the equivalent in music of the conversation of old ladies at a tea party." This being the case, I should suppose smiles would develop into chuckles when you came across a certain newspaper obituary—" Mr. —— was one of the last survivors of the band of musicians who formerly occupied the west gallery of the church. In this he for years did double service, simultaneously singing tenor and playing the bassoon."

You with your knowledge and ability would be able when you saw an announcement of Mr. Szymanovski's violin piece, " Dryads et Pan," intelligently to anti-cipate that the part of the piece descriptive of the first-named would be marked " col legno," and to be

disappointed when this did not occur. And you were
kind in your comment when, in the report of a recent
case, you read : " On the night of October 8, at 11.30,
Coxall saw Brown enter the house with Harris. Soon
afterwards the music upstairs started ; the piano was
loudly played, and there was noisy dancing, which
continued until 12.15, when the ' Dead March ' was
played in a very loud key and with one finger."
People at large do not understand these simple matters,
as I am constantly finding. One day I gave a simple
lecture, illustrated by a piano quartet ; I drew attention to the instruments, and had each played separately,
so that the difference of tone might be grasped and
the weaving of the parts more intelligently followed.
A member of the audience afterwards wrote : " The
piece is written for Violin, Violoncello, Piola, and
Piano," which suggests a reflection upon my articulation, but at the same time reveals the general ignorance
of musical fact and terminology even amongst those
who love our art enough to come and hear it talked
about. Partly this is the fault of those of us who
write about music in the newspapers, and those others
who compile annotated programmes, for keeping ourselves so consistently above the heads of a big section
of our public, and never condescending to explain the
terms in use, with the consequence that such writings
cease to be read by those who most need them, and
the wider public remains uninstructed.

Talking of Annotated Programmes, what do you
think would be the really useful way of writing them ?
For I am sure that in their present form they are
largely wasted. I dare not say much on this subject

just now, for almost all these productions are the work
of my respected and friendly colleagues. But here is
one by a very good composer, descriptive of his own
new work, which was to be performed for the first
time. One may always poke fun at a composer (indeed,
this is a critic's business), and so I will ask my friend
who wrote this how many people in his large audience,
in his judgment, enjoyed his admirable work the more
for having put into their hands this solid chunk of a
Table of Contents. Nay—how many even read it ?

The principal theme (a) on which the whole poem
is built is given out in the Introduction, first on muted
Horns, then on the Clarinet. This is followed by a
small but important motif (b), played by 'Cello solo
and answered by the Violas. A condensed form of
theme (a), worked in with (b) during *accelerando*,
brings us to the *Allegro*. The motif of the *Allegro* (c)
is founded on the principal theme (a). This motif,
or slight variations of it, brings us to the *Andante*,
which is formed on theme (b) and is given out by the
Clarinet. At the end of the *Andante* the themes (c)
and (b) form the development, and theme (a) is also
heard on Strings. A descending motif (d) from the
Allegro is used for the climax, which is quickly followed by a recapitulation of the *Allegro* very much
condensed. The *Andante* motif is this time played
by the Strings and accompanied by Trombones, and,
later, triplets played by Horns form an important
counterpoint. A motif (e) is formed from end of the
Andante and given out by Wood-wind. This works
up to a *Stretto*, which, gradually quickening, prepares
entrance of chief theme given out by six Horns in
unison. A further *Stretto* brings us to *Finale*, giving
forth theme (e) by Horns and Trumpets in Octaves.

But I have strayed a little from my original intention, which was to set that headmaster and my readers a useful and interesting " Christmas Holiday Employment." All that now remains for me to do is to announce that no prize is offered for the most complete and correct solution of my little series of Christmas conundrums. Nor should the workings of the paper be sent to me. You must be your own examiners.

V. Our Pauper Public

The criticism I am now going to make concerns a feature of musical life in London, and, so far as I know, of musical life nowhere in this country but London. We have in London two definite publics for music—the paying public and the pauper public. The latter has been deliberately brought into existence by concert-givers and (especially) concert-agents, and I suggest its entire abolition, since, from what I hear (and I have made some rather careful inquiries), I believe that in the long run this public is of little use to concert-givers or concert-agents, and certainly of no use to music. The large non-paying public for music has come about in this way. A. B. decides to give a piano recital, a vocal recital, or an orchestral concert. He engages C. D., a concert agent, to arrange it for him. It is recognized from the first that A. B.'s drawing powers are insufficient to fill the hall. C. D. therefore advises him that a number of tickets should be distributed. When the event takes place the small paying public arrives and passes into the hall, the pauper public, which has received free passes, unsolicited, by post, crowds round the box-office and exchanges them for actual numbered tickets. Sometimes the thing is underdone and the hall is still unfilled ; just occasionally it is overdone and aggrieved persons holding free passes are turned away. This system is the full explanation of several overflowing audiences lately in various London halls, and, as I think, the partial explanation of several grossly insufficient audiences. I have seen the Queen's Hall filled this season for an indifferent performer, and half empty the same week for an excellent one of great reputation, for the front-rank performer who demands payment cannot always successfully compete with the second-rank performer who does not.

The custom of free distribution is of long standing, but has lately, I think, become more open.   I am told it is by no means uncommon now for persons who wish to attend a particular concert boldly to write to the agent, begging for free passes, whilst others who have a mere general wish to attend concerts make the more general request : " Will you kindly add my name to your free list ? "   The admission of the existence of a free list is often made by concert organizations you would not suspect of possessing or needing such a thing by announcements in the papers on special occasions, " Free List Entirely Suspended," and once lately, at the recital of a front-rank performer who would certainly have drawn a paying audience but for the previous pauperization of a large section of the musical public, an attendant was stationed in the vestibule to cry openly "This way to the free seats ! "   So nice in its tastes and exacting in its demands is the free public now becoming that many of its members will turn up their noses at events of minor importance, or seats in an inferior position, and an agent lately remarked to me bitterly that soon it would become necessary to offer not merely free places but also free cars to fetch the audience and a free supper afterwards. The scriptural injunction as to going into the highways and hedges is almost literally fulfilled, for I have heard of agents giving their employees batches of tickets to distribute to the waitresses at the tea shops they frequent and to the clerks at the post office they use. The whole system has reached monstrous proportions. It is quite undignified and, I think, uncommercial.

To a performer beginning public life I would say— forbid the gift of a single ticket to the general public. You may intend merely to do so for your first recital or two, but having once begun the practice you will find yourself almost compelled to keep it up, lest, as you will say, "People may think that my public is dropping off." Begin boldly with whatever small public you can get, and, if your gifts are what you think them to be, it will grow. The presence of the larger non-paying public deceives nobody. Every music critic, as he enters, casts his eye at once over your hall, recognizes the type of person present, and says, with a sniff, "Well-papered!" The non-payers, of course, not only know themselves to be such, but imagine all their neighbours to be the same. The honest people who have, like men, paid down their two-and-four or their five-and-nine to hear you, know quite well the class of people that surrounds them, and are offended, just as you yourself are when, having paid for the comfort of first-class travel on the railway, you find your carriage filled with those who have not so paid. So the unwise concert-giver, by his excessive generosity, gains no man's favour and some men's contempt.

Concert-agents might well look at the custom in this way—the people on their free lists are either real music-lovers or they are not. If they are real music-lovers they would in any case attend a certain number of concerts per month and pay for them ; the price of the tickets given to such people represents, then, a deduction from actual London concert receipts. If they are not music-lovers they make a bad audience for the performer, and, as a matter of fact, it is notorious that a great part of a free-list audience takes too little interest in the music even to buy programmes, or, if these are free, hardly troubles to follow them, being present simply for the mild entertainment of a night out.

There are two things that are called for if good concerts are to be made to pay again : (a) completely to abolish these " dead-heads," and (b) to reduce costs of concert-giving. The abolition of the free-lister can only be done effectively by a combination of concert-agents. Will they combine ? How to bring about a reduction of costs they know better than I, but I think the position would be simplified if we had one or two well-placed and well-appointed halls smaller than our present halls with their necessarily high rents. Further, lower entrance charges would, I think, help to increase audiences. The middle-class music-lover cannot nowadays afford the frequent expenditure of even three-and-sixpence, plus sixpence or a shilling for a mere sheet or two of paper as programme, the fares from and to his home, and perhaps a necessary meal in town ; and when his family includes another musical member or two whom he wishes to take with him the event of a concert visit to central London has to be a rare one. If, having abolished our non-paying public, and turned some portion of it again into a paying public, it is still quite impossible to get sufficiently big audiences together to make concerts remunerative, I suggest that it would be better to incur the inevitable deficit by reducing prices all round. Let everybody pay *something* to enter, rather than admit a large section of the audience free and so entirely "spoil" them for the future.

VI. THE ETHICS OF APPLAUSE

Sometimes, at the end of a week, looking back over that week's experiences, I recall my astonishment at some of them and come to the conclusion that this astonishment is a clear proof of my being afflicted with an incorrigible naivety. Again and again there happens something which I have seen happen dozens of times before, yet which comes to me afresh as startling and incredible. Such a shock was mine one week-end as I recalled a certain concert of the London Chamber Concert Society, at which a young player performed very badly three pieces of Chopin and won such a round of applause as compelled an encore. I cannot remember that I have heard this player before or since, and must not be understood as reflecting upon his general standard. For all I know, his habitual Chopin-playing may entitle him to be regarded as a veritable Pachmann - Godovsky - Moiseivitch ; all I now say about him must be understood as referring strictly to his playing on the occasion in question, which I found

to be rigidly wooden, lacking in feeling, lacking in full-
ness of tone, lacking in climax, and indeed entirely
amateurish. Perhaps I heard him on one of the " off
days " to which every artist.is exposed, and should my
next experience of his playing be more fortunate it will
be a real pleasure to me to report the fact. Indeed,
though the hearing of Chopin, as passed through his
hands, was on this occasion trying, I quarrel not with
him but with his admirers, who seemed, after years of
the hearing of Chopin-playing by pianists of every
nation and every school, to be still entirely without a
standard by which to guide their judgment. In considering this phenomenon we must not overlook the
fact that the audience which gathers to hear the programmes of this excellent society is usually taken as an
intelligent and instructed one ; indeed, the programmes
are not drafted in such a way as to appeal to the " man
in the street."

Can it be, however, that we over-rate the intelligence
and critical ability even of such an audience as this ?
Is such an audience in reality made up of George
Dyers ?   You remember Lamb's remarks on his friend,
who had " an utter incapacity for comprehending that
there can be anything bad in poetry."   " All poems
are good poems to George ; all men are fine geniuses."
Substitute " pianism " for " poetry," and " playing "
for " poems," and you have, apparently, a description
of the mind, not indeed of the whole of this pianist's
audience (for I saw a few very wry faces here and
there), but, say, of nine-tenths of it. If we are to take
applause as the barometer of our national musical
weather, we must often be distressed to find the read-

ings so low. With all due respect I would say that the
ladies seemed to me to be the most at fault on the day of
which I am writing, and the awful thought struck me
that perhaps we have still a population of Mrs. Bayham
Badgers. You remember the lady—" surrounded in
her drawing-room by various objects indicative of
playing the piano a little, playing the guitar a little,
singing a little, working a little, reading a little, writing
poetry a little, botanizing a little." Can that be the
sort of person the Chamber Concert Society attracts ?
I cannot believe it ; there must be some other explanation. Yet we have it on the authority of a recent
issue of " Truth " that " a good deal of the art of
concert-giving consists in persuading people who do
not want to go to concerts into the belief that
they cannot socially afford not to be seen at
them."

Another possible theory is that our audience's applause was insincere. I do not adopt this theory, but
I throw out for what it is worth the suggestion that a
good deal of insincerity does lie behind a good deal of
applause. Pursuing my curious investigations into the
general subject at a concert a few weeks earlier, I went
up to a group of our young composers, who were very
violently applauding some thoroughly bad violin-
playing, and begged them to tell me their motive.
" Hush ! " said one of them in a mysterious whisper,
putting his mouth close to my ear, and looking round
with furtive anxiety, " Diplomatic reasons—near
vicinity ! " I retired sadly, recalling that this same
young composer had come up to me, in the vestibule
before the concert, and cheered my critical heart with

approval of my previous Sunday's article, with which, he assured me, he entirely and warmly agreed. One does sometimes get these little unintended slaps, but my real worry about that young composer was like Beethoven's about the cook he dismissed—" Whoever tells a lie is not pure of heart, and such a person cannot cook a clean soup."

I have got a horrid feeling that composers are often insincere in their applause. We may not have in this country what Dame Ethel Smyth longs for under the name of " The Machine," but we have got a great many wheels within wheels, and I rather think these young people became badly involved in their dizzy revolution. It must be difficult, for instance, to refuse to applaud a conductor who has just directed a performance of a rotten work when you know he is at the moment considering giving a much finer one of your own, or a singer who has just sung badly but who helped you in your early days by giving your works " a show." And then it is so much easier after a concert to go up to your composer-colleague, clap him on the back, and say " Jolly good, old chap ! " than to keep out of his way and show by your silence your real opinion. There is, indeed, even the danger that if you do this latter your honesty may be taken for jealousy, and that the good-fellowship of the artistic life may suffer. The result of all this, I imagine, is that, amongst composers, the currency of applause has become debased. I should guess that even young composers soon come to think rather little of the praise of their fellows—except, of course, those two or three quite exceptional ones who have themselves a really

high opinion of their own work, and these, we may
suppose, will swallow anything.

Applause, genuine applause, worthily bestowed, is a
valuable tonic. The health of our musical life depends
on the purity of the article and on its proper adminis-
tration. Take the case with which I opened as an
example. Assuming that the player was on that occasion " off his form," we have given him the impression
that this does not matter, and that in future he need
pay no special heed to his preparation of his work.
But assuming that he has too much intelligence and
artistic idealism to be influenced in that way, we have
then taken from him his faith in our judgment, and
so watered down our tonic that our future doses of it
will fail to stimulate. Lastly, assuming (as I hope I
ought not to do) that the playing we heard was the
player's normal best, then we have done a gross injustice
to a dozen young players who can do better, who would
give a great deal for the chance of appearing before
such an audience, and who will perhaps never have the
chance of doing this if we show the organizers of these
concerts that the inferior article satisfies us. This last
consideration weighs with me very heavily. There
are all around us so many young pianists, violinists,
singers, and composers awaiting trial that we do a
great wrong by encouraging those who have already
come to trial and, in the minds of any just judge and
jury, lost their case. Remember that the courts are
grossly overcrowded, and the cause-list a long one.

And now, turning from this question of the ethics
of applause as they affect performers, I wish once
more just to touch on a point which involves justice

to the works performed. Writing recently of the performance by the Sevcik Quartet of Beethoven's Opus 135, I said quite rudely and bluntly, " It is surely undignified on the part of four artists of such standing to break the course of their performance of a great work in order that they may bow like well-tipped waiters showing out a guest." I received a few days later this letter from Dr. Adrian Boult : " I support most strongly your remarks about applause. Why Amsterdam and Cologne should be the only towns that never applaud between the movements of a work I cannot make out. The amazingly effective key-relationships in Brahms and many other composers are completely ruined by the interruption of applause. Surely most artists will agree with you."

WHAT THE PUBLIC WANTS

I. " BEASTLY TUNES "

ONE of the most active discussions upon a musical
subject that any of us can recall took place
recently. It arose out of Sir Hugh Allen's bold condemnation of " filthy tunes." This was immediately
taken up as a challenge by Mr. Herman Darewski.
The views of both these active musical workers were
at once reported by almost every paper in the country.
Snappy paragraphs and serious leading articles were
written upon them, the correspondence columns of
the daily Press bore witness to the interest they had
aroused, the musical Press discussed the big question
which had at last been so boldly and publicly raised.
There was probably a general feeling on both sides that
it was a good thing that an opportunity should at last
have come about of getting to grips and trying to
achieve a public settlement of mind upon a vital question. For the question is really vital. It matters
infinitely more to the country what view the general
public ultimately takes upon this question of popular
tune than what view it takes upon the work of Scriabin
or Stravinsky or Holst or Goossens or the Paris " Six."
It is, indeed, the very key-question of musical life. I
do not know whether I may claim to be musically

impartial—which of us is ? But so far as the main
personalities engaged in this dispute are concerned I
can. Both parties are personal friends. I have spent
many an hour in Mr. Darewski's palatial popular publishing office in Charing Cross Road, and, equally, I
have had many a chat with Sir Hugh in the Director's
room at the Royal College of Music, and at Oxford,
where he is Professor of Music. I do not believe
that either party would readily take offence at anything I might say, and I will venture on a few
remarks.

Firstly I would say that if Sir Hugh maintains that
all popular tunes are bad I think he is wrong. I do
not believe he does, but some people have taken his
remarks in that way. Thus Mr. Darewski himself
says :

" I presume he referred to such ' beastly ' tunes
as ' Keep the Home Fires Burning,' ' The Long, Long
Trail,' ' Tipperary,' ' Sister Susie,' and ' Pack up
your Troubles in your old Kit Bag.' "

Well, " Pack up your Troubles " helped to win the
war. The days have gone by for tall talk about the
war, but I do believe that this tune, with its cheery
words, was worth several hundred thousand men to
the British Army. When everything was wrong some
incurable optimist would strike up the song, and the
sun would shine again. That tune worked miracles.
And it is a " good " tune, and so is " Tipperary." Mr.
Darewski (who is, perhaps, reading these lines at the
same moment as you) knows who Sir Walford Davies
is, for I remember in a conversation during the war

mentioning his R.A.F. song stunts, whereupon, in the most comical way Mr. Darewski put his hands together in a mock-devotional attitude and said, " Walford Davies—oh, that's the chap who gets on a platform before the soldiers and says (imitating, in a sancti-monious voice) : *Let us now sing Fugue One Hundred and Seventy-eight.*" Mr. Darewski will remember the incident. His clever imaginary impersonation made me roar, and very likely Walford Davies (who, like Mr. Darewski himself, is a " good sport ") will do the same when he reads this record of it.

We now come to something that will interest Mr. Darewski. In the old " Tipperary " days, when every one was singing the thing, and when, as he would think, the fugue-loving, high-browed Sir Walford Davies would be driven to putting cotton-wool in his ears in the impossibility of escaping otherwise from something really " popular," I heard him cry, in a committee meeting, with the music critic of " The Times " in the chair, and Sir Hugh Allen's predecessor as Director of the Royal College of Music, Sir Hubert Parry, sitting beside him—" ' Tipperary ! ' I'd be *proud* to have written such a tune ! " But, as Dame Ethel Smyth once said, " The difference between ' Tipperary ' and the vulgar music-hall ditties that have a passing vogue, is as the difference between a perfect French omelette and the English lodging-house variety." The point I am making is obvious. Mr. Darewski is to recognize that there are popular tunes *and* popular tunes. Some are popular and good and some are popular and bad. And when they are good I do not suppose Sir Hugh Allen is a bit behind Sir Walford Davies or Mr. Darewski himself in rejoicing that they are popular. But they must be good !

So we have established the fact that Mr. Darewski and Co. on the one hand, and Sir Hugh Allen and Co. on the other, have some common ground. They actually share approval of the very latest " popular " tunes when they happen to be " good." After the passage above quoted, Mr. Darewski goes on to say :

" Army commanders, recruiting officers, hospital commandants, and Sir Arthur Yapp would probably have something to say in regard to the baleful influence Sir Hugh Allen appears to think they (popular tunes) exercise upon the moral fibre of the public at large."

With recruiting officers I unfortunately never had official relations. My own impression in 1914 and 1915 was that they did not for a moment realize, as Mr. Darewski and Sir Hugh Allen and I myself do, the stimulating value of music. Of " army commanders " and hospital commandants I could tell Mr. Darewski quite a lot, and of Sir Arthur Yapp I will actually venture to give a little personal anecdote. During the war, the Y.M.C.A., having the impression that some of my musical experiences with the army in France might be in some way suggestive, asked me to address its National Council. We met in the Tottenham Court Road building, and after prayer and preliminaries, I was called upon. I fear I used some violent, almost Allen-like language in describing the sort of music the Association was then providing for the troops abroad. But my oratorical torrent was broken in the middle by Sir Arthur Yapp himself, who exclaimed, " But you

must admit, Mr. Scholes, that the men *like* that sort
of thing." I sought for a retort, and (in Y.M.C.A.
phrase) the Lord gave me the right word. " If your
principle is to give the men what they like, Sir Arthur,
provide beer in your huts! " Whereupon fifty solemn
Y.M.C.A. faces broke into a grin and Sir Arthur's bore
the broadest.

Of course the soldiers did like " beastly " and
" filthy " music. They liked any kind of music they
could get. Men do ! Its mere rhythm is a physical
stimulus. But experience showed that they liked
" good " just as much as " bad." Mr. Darewski antici-
pated me here, and, in a newspaper interview, admitting that " nice " tunes given by the more artistic concert parties were received with enthusiasm, he says,
" Yes, but did the men *sing them ?* " Here is an extract from a letter I lately received from a reader. It
bears on the point, I think :

I am glad that you realize the admirable work
that the gramophone is doing. I remember, during
the war, playing string-quartets to a mess-room
otherwise occupied in playing bridge. Result : Sixteen non-musical, but absorbent minds find themselves subconsciously laden with, as the adjutant
remarked, " queer little sticky scraps," and whistle
them all day long. This is a fact.

A reader of the " Pall Mall " wrote, soon after the
war, that his experience was that " ' Annie Laurie '
had no rival in the military camps." I disagree—and
say " Loch Lomond." And these two tunes come
rather near the class Mr. Darewski derides when he

imagines the knightly Sir Hugh " grasping the flaming sword " and crying " Banish popular music from our schools and streets and substitute folk-songs and modal melodies of bygone days ! " Does Mr. Darewski remember a very " popular " song of a few years since, " A Little Bit Off the Top " ? This was simply a revival of the good old " When Johnny Comes Marching Home." " The Sheeny Man " was a fine tune, and, in its simple way, the chorus of " Tara-ra-boom-de-ay " was, I think, not bad, nor was dear old " Daisy " when you come to think of it. Let Mr. Darewski, then, compose or publish a few songs of this class, and he will do good and make money ! And talking of street pianos (as both Mr. Darewski and Sir Hugh Allen do), only a couple of years ago there was one which haunted Bloomsbury whose repertory included several old English morris dances. All these things are " good," yet they are quite " popular." Indeed, I believe that the Darewski-Yapp theory is wrong. The " people " may not understand *complex music* without opportunities of familiarizing themselves with it, but they do not demand *bad* music. I think, however, with Sir Hugh, that to-day they are getting a good deal of the latter and feel sure that the " popular " tunes we now hear are nothing like so artistically " good " as those of twenty years ago. This may be but the glamour which old age casts around the memories of youth—but I believe not ! We are in Mr. Darewski's hands. Let us admit that he can do a hundred times more for British music from Charing Cross Road than can Sir Hugh Allen from Prince Consort Road. Will he do it ?

II. THE POPULAR PROGRAMME

Not long ago I had the pleasure of attending two
London orchestral concerts for " the people "—on
Saturday night Mr. John H. Foulds' at the St. George's
Hall (Central Y.M.C.A., Tottenham Court Road), and
on Sunday afternoon Mr. Adrian Boult's at the People's
Palace, in the Mile End Road. Mr. Foulds' programme
was of the better light-music class. It included
Thomas's " Raymond " overture, a " Tannhäuser "
Fantasia, the conductor's own " Keltic Suite," the
Stanford-Grainger " Irish Reel " (piano solo), etc., and
some songs. Mr. Boult's consisted of three pieces only,
all orchestral, of which Vaughan Williams's " London
Symphony " was the centre. Mr. Foulds' concert, in
its comparatively small hall, I found to be well attended
by an enthusiastic audience : Mr. Boult's audience was
at least equally enthusiastic, but his very large hall
was insufficiently filled, and those present evidently
came largely not from the immediate neighbourhood,
for which his series was intended, but from more or less
distant and " respectable " suburbs. The announcement was made during the afternoon that the average
attendance during the season had been but 600, that
an average of 1,800 was necessary to pay bare expenses,
and that the governors of the Palace felt obliged to
defer the remaining three concerts of the series until
the autumn, so that the expected loss upon them might
fall into another financial year. So far as I can recall
these concerts were given, and then the scheme was
entirely dropped. Artistically, Mr. Boult and his
British Symphony Orchestra are admitted to have

gloriously succeeded ; financially, they failed, receiving, I am sure, the warmest sympathy of every music-lover.

The biggest factor deciding between success and failure in any popular series is, of course, the composition of the programmes. The common-sense view which is often expressed is this—" You must begin right down where the people already are, and pull them up with you." Provided there is no misunderstanding as to the interpretation of the words " where the people are," I support this view. But the idea that you are to begin with " bad " music, proceed to " better," and at last arrive at " good " is erroneous. The " people " do not love bad music because it is bad (some bad music they do not love at all), but because it possesses some " popular " qualities. This principle, which applies to every form of art, including literature, has been admirably laid down by Mr. Chesterton in his book on Dickens :

I may perhaps ask leave to examine this fashionable statement—the statement that the public likes bad literature, and even likes literature because it is bad. This way of stating the thing is an error. The public does not like bad literature. The public likes a certain kind of literature, and likes that kind of literature even when it is bad better than another kind of literature even when it is good. Nor is this unreasonable ; for the line between different types of literature is as real as the line between tears and laughter ; and to tell people who can only get bad comedy that you have some first-class tragedy is as irrational as to offer a man who is shivering over weak, warm coffee a really superior sort of ice.

Later, the writer actually applies this to music :

When they walk behind the brass of the Salvation Army band, instead of listening to the harmonies at Queen's Hall, it is always assumed that they prefer bad music. But it may be merely that they prefer military music, music marching down the open street, and that if Dan Godfrey's band could be smitten with salvation and lead them they would like that even better.

In these extracts we have, I think, our principle clearly suggested. We are to " give the people what they want," but we can do so without going outside the field of good music. Let me draw an illustration from the programme of Mr. Foulds' concert, where it was generally, though not quite completely, observed. Here Miss Megan Foster sang the Hebridean " Fairy's Love Song " (from Mrs. Kennedy-Fraser's collection), and " Dashing away with the smoothing iron " (from Mr. Cecil Sharp's) ; and she also sang " Voi che sapete," and songs by Stanford and Quilter, but none of those cheap " ballads " which many consider indispensable at a popular concert. She had as good a reception as any singer could wish. The popular audience loves " tunes," and she gave them tunes ; had she given them bad tunes they would have been satisfied, but she gave them good ones, and, sung in her pleasant, clear voice, with the words carefully but naturally enunciated, these were equally acceptable. Similarly the public likes waltzes, so Mr. Foulds gave them the Strauss " Doctrinen " set. He might have given them some of the popular Charing Cross Road cheapnesses of the moment, and they would probably have been satisfied, but he had grasped the Chestertonian principle, and he acted upon it with perfect success. As a matter of fact, the " begin with bad music and lead on to good " people altogether forget the existence of an enormous body of music, the love of which is common to the man in the street and the musician : to give but a few examples, Grieg's first " Peer Gynt " suite, Bizet's " L'Arlésienne " suite, Tchaikovsky's " Nutcracker " suite, much Wagner, and some Beethoven (if given at first in smallish quantities). Whether there is in existence enough good literature of the kind the " people " love I do not know, but I am of opinion that there is enough good orchestral music of this kind for all " popular concert " purposes, i.e., music with (a) tune and rhythm, (b) bold orchestral colouring, and (c) simple emotion vividly expressed.

Why, then, did Mr. Boult meet with his disappointing setback ? Not because his music was too good, but because some of it has not been of the particular kind that will attract and hold the Mile Ender. To begin with, a mere three-piece programme does not give the variety a musical public still in its child-mind state demands, and, moreover, does not provide the same likelihood of confronting it on the bills with the name of something it already knows and accepts, either through hearing it at the " pictures " or on the gramophone. (In order to leave room for variety I see no objection whatever to performing single movements of symphonic works at concerts such as this.) Then it was perhaps a mistake not to include the solo element. There is nothing to which the most fastidious of us can object about a fine singer with a good song or two, or a violinist or pianist playing a single movement from a great concerto. The big public which Mr. Boult wishes to attract loves a singer and it loves an instrumental soloist ; let it have what it loves and, having got it there to enjoy that, you can gradually train it to enjoy other things that you, perhaps, love even better. Concessions are called for. We are to step down—not from the good to bad, but from the long to the short, the involved to the simple, the more serious to the less so. We can give just as good music as before, but some of it will be of another kind of goodness and each programme will provide goodness in six or eight varieties instead of (at most) three. In this most excellent series of concerts we began with long symphonies in our first season and should have come to them in our third. It is easy to be wise after the event—and that is all I am professing to be !

"FOR THE GOOD OF MUSIC"

THE music critic is always causing trouble. It
is, I think, an agreed fact amongst our craft
that no one of our number ever yet wrote an article
or concert notice that did not get some one on the
raw. The following incident will illustrate the point.
A short time ago, discussing " The Planets," which
was then a novelty, I quite innocently stated, on the
sound authority of an eye-witness, that when " Jupiter, the Bringer of Jollity " was first rehearsed, " the
Queen's Hall charwomen were found to have put down
their brooms and buckets, and to be dancing in the
corridors." May " Venus, the Bringer of Peace "
henceforth guide my pen, for here is the condemnation
my remark brought :

QUEEN'S HALL,
November 18, 1920.

(To be printed.)

EDITOR,

I think it is a pity Mr. Percy A. Scholes did not
keep his criticism to music and left the Charwomen
as he calls them out, for he might have got them
discharged. The Charwomen are a body of women,
hard worked, turning up at all times to suit the public,
Sundays included. . . . You will see the Women

have no time to dance, as it may yet make trouble, so I ask Mr. Percy Scholes to keep to music in future and leave

The Queen's Hall
Dustie Fairies Alone
FAIRPLAY.

I may say that I have reason to believe this protest a genuine communication from the source from which it professes to come, and I hereby fully and unreservedly apologize to a conscientious and diligent body of workers without whose morning labours our evening pleasures would be much impaired. And in token of contrition I have here given their complaint, omitting only some technical explanation of the difficult conditions under which their public-spirited work is conducted. (I cannot but think that history records some previous instance of a dignified protest of this kind. What is it? It runs in my head that it concerned Mr. Spectator and the man who played the lion at the opera.)

But seriously, now, whilst we are in this field cannot we harvest a useful thought or two? Can music have any better end than to awaken an emotional response in the minds of hard-working men and women? Holst himself, who associated in youth with William Morris, in later years organized music at a University Settlement, during the war went out to Salonica and Constantinople to teach soldiers to sing Byrd and Dowland, and every week of his life trains choir and orchestra at a working-people's college on the unfashionable side of the river, would, I think, give us a quick answer to the question. Music is to him a social force, I feel sure—not a refined amusement for a special little group of Royal Collegians and Royal Academicians and cultured amateurs and (cultured or uncultured ?) music critics. If not everybody has the chance of hearing what this composer writes that is a question of something wrong with our social conditions—not with his musical intentions. I think Holst would probably take more pleasure in that story of the women dancing to " Jupiter " than in a good criticism in " The Times " or " The Observer."

What is your theory as to the purpose of music ? We are constantly asked to give money or service for " the good of music " or to join societies for " the good of British music." But we observe that " the good of music " generally seems to mean " the good of composers." It is right that we should help these people, and, especially, save them from the deadening effect of discouragement in their earlier stages of effort ; Holst himself has perhaps lost about ten years of his life through the delay of the full recognition that is now coming to him, and in a properly organized society he would have been saved this loss. But to work for " the good of music," meaning the good of the composer, is like supporting a missionary society for " the good of " the missionaries, or the boy-scout organization, meaning Sir Baden Powell, or St. Dunstan's, meaning Sir Arthur Pearson's efficient successors. In any case, " the good of music " is a meaningless phrase. Music cannot be " done good to " ; it can only do good—or harm. It is not a passive recipient but an active agent.

Just how music does good or harm is vague to us

because psychology is still an imperfect and inexact science. The theory, I suppose, is that man actually has something which can be called a " soul," that this soul is capable of development in all sorts of directions, that the more it develops the better for the man, that certain sorts of music have a " truth " about them and others have not, that the " true " music is food and the make-believe merely husks—and so forth. Nobody can as yet prove the correctness of such a theory, but anyone who has experienced either, on the one hand, the development of a general enjoyment or interest in music, or, on the other, a gradual change of taste from " bad " to " good," knows that the development or the change meant to him a growth. Incidentally, whilst thinking of this question of " good " and " bad " music, remember the significance of the fact that whilst thousands could testify to a change of taste from " bad " to " good," probably never yet one could tell us that his taste has changed from " good " to " bad." That fact must be admitted as evidence for a vital distinction as to values that plenty of people still deny. So it all comes down to this, that work for " the good of music " is a form of social propaganda, and should be encouraged and supported, financially and otherwise, by the same earnest people who encourage and support the efforts of the S.P.G. or the Scout movement or St. Dunstan's. I confess that I see no reason in giving money or work merely for " the good of music." " Music for Music's sake " is not a tenable theory of the purpose of musical life.

Sincerity, depth and beauty are, so far as I can see, the three great qualities to be looked for in the music

we ought to support.   There is not a word to be said
for insincere music.   Its composer is to be blamed.
And as for shallow music, its composer is to be not
blamed but pitied and gently put on one side.   What
constitutes beauty is, of course, a question leaving
room for debate, though we all know well enough
what we mean by the requirement.   There is the
fourth quality of being well made, but this is a minor
and matter-of-course demand, and this quality is only
an essential because badly made music, however " sincere " or however " deep " or however " beautiful,"
will not last, and is, therefore, not worth our spending
our time over.   A word may be needed to guard the
expression " deep " from misunderstanding ; it is
only included to provide against that class of composers whose intention is " sincere," but whose natures
are academic, on the one hand, or shallow and sentimental on the other.   It really means nothing more
than that music shall not be either stodgy or trivial,
though it may be either serious or " light."   And,
speaking of shallowness, the weakening effect of the
popular " drawing-room ballad " is probably a phenomenon worthy of the attention of statesmen.   And
here, of course, I have Plato with me—or, more
modestly put, I am with Plato.

WHETHER hens exist in order to bring forth eggs, or eggs in order to bring forth hens, is a question never yet answered by science. Whether composers exist in order to provide the public with music, or the public in order to provide occupation and encouragement for composers, is another question about which many people (and particularly writers on music) still seem a little hazy. For myself I have no doubt at all, as you will have gathered from the brief treatment of the subject under the heading "For the Good of Music," in which I plumped for the public as the beneficiaries and the composers as the benefactors. Yet people will for a long time ask us to go on supporting concert schemes and British Music Societies and the like "for the good of music," and, after all, it does not much matter, since you cannot well have either hens without eggs or eggs without hens. There is an enormous lot of Missionary Zeal for music floating about at present, and whether it be directed towards making the world safe for composers or helping composers to save the world its object comes to much the same. All musicians realize that something wants doing, and, on the one hand, they get up Patron's Funds for performing composers' works and Carnegie schemes for publishing them, and, on the other, People's Concert Societies and Concert Decentralization schemes for giving a wider public the chance of listening. Both sorts of activity are necessary, but for myself I lay the stress, as I have just hinted, on the needs of the public rather than on the needs of the composers, for that is where I think the strain is just now most acute. Until we train a really big audience to appreciate music I do not see how composers are to live, so even those who think more of the needs of the composer than of the needs of the public can join with me in an urgent plea for the education of the public. This education I look upon as *the* problem of the coming ten years. And so, I am happy to think, do a good many other people.

When there first appeared the article, " What does the Audience hear ? " (see page 3) I heard from several correspondents who capped my cases of ill-timed applause by some of their own. One lady actually told me of a Wigmore Hall audience which had that very week interrupted Beethoven's " Adieux " Sonata (of all well-known pieces !) by applause at the wrong place, and in the following letter a well-known pianist told of another atrocity :

" In illustration to your article about the musicality of certain audiences the most flagrant thing I ever heard was when Eugen d'Albert once played in Geneva (Switzerland), supposed to be a musical town, the F minor Fantasia of Chopin.

" Before the slow episode in B major, the former matter is brought to the conclusion by an arpeggio figure and then closes in G flat. At that moment there was such a storm of applause that d'Albert

never finished the Fantasy. The same thing hap-
pened to me at Southsea, with the difference that
I finished the Fantasy, as I tried to indicate, by a
gesture of the hand meaning, *More to come!*
"Yours faithfully,
"CERNIKOFF."

These lapses seem at first unpardonable. It appears
strange that no pianist, however eminent, can be sure
of obtaining a proper hearing for any work of any
composer, however well known he may think it. And
the curious thing is that it is the very enthusiasts that
offend. If the disasters took the character of deliberate
inattention during the performance of a masterpiece
we could, perhaps, blame the audience. As it is we
must pity them—and set to work to educate them.

To blame an audience for not following a work
intelligently seems to me to be in itself an unintelli-
gent proceeding. Just how to prevent catastrophes
of the particular kind I have been talking about I do
not know. Perhaps a sort of "Please do not get off
until the bus stops!" note on the programme, might
be some good, or we might have an official applause
leader, like the man who supervises and organizes the
yelling at an American college baseball match. But
in the long run nothing but solid education will fully
serve our purpose. And we ought to take these little
occurrences as symptoms. If those who do come to
a concert show so little understanding, how many do
you suppose have stayed away because they knew
the music was going to be over their heads? It is
only by a wide education in music that we shall get
our concert halls filled.

Take almost any work you care to name (any but
the very simplest) and you will find that it contains
certain vital passages that are miles above the head
of the ordinary listener.   Take, for instance, Scriabin's
" Divine Poem."   How does the plain man appreciate
this ?   Well, of course, he is carried away here and
there by the magnificent *entrain* of the piece.
And he can follow its general moods—the mood of
striving of one of the subjects, the mood of solemn
elevation of another, a sense of the " mystérieux,
romantique, légendaire " (to quote the composer's
own score) in a third.   But when Scriabin combines
all three of these subjects who knows that he has done
so ? . . .   A very few people who have bought scores
and who have studied them well beforehand.   Here
is the combination (I have not at the moment my
score at hand, but I think I am right in saying that
the uppermost theme is given to the first violins, the
middle one to the second violins, and the bottom one
to the string basses : an accompanying part for the
violas is left out here, as not bearing on the matter
under discussion :

I venture to say that nine out of ten of my readers
will need to do a little practical ear-sharpening work
with that passage before they can hear the three
themes at once.   Try to grasp the passage as a friend

plays it to you on the piano. If you cannot hear the three simultaneous themes, get him to play each of them separately several times and then try again until you do. After this simple experiment you will realize what the more ordinary person (ungifted with your strong natural musical sense and trained musical intelligence) is bound to miss when he hears a symphonic work. We may take it that Scriabin had both a formal and a poetical purpose in this combination of themes. You perhaps may attach more importance to the latter purpose than to the former, but how on earth is the latter purpose to be served if the former is unrealized? I am sure I do not know, and it seems to me that we must either join in the cry of Tolstoi (in his "What is Art?") and demand that our composers should reduce their works to the greatest simplicity, or else that we must educate our audiences.

To quote from Scriabin may be to give the impression that it is modern music that offers these difficulties for the hearer. But it is only a matter of degree, and not a wide degree either. Bach is as Bax and Scarlatti almost as Scriabin to the plain man. There are plenty of simple pieces which the plain man can enjoy straight away, but as soon as the composer begins to dive at all deep he leaves the plain man gasping on the surface. And even in the pieces which the plain man does more or less enjoy there is a lot he misses. There are some of the Bach fugues so rollicking or so solemn that anyone can enjoy them, in a sort of way, as mere mood-pictures, but to get out of them all the pleasure Bach meant you to get you must have a little knowledge and listening skill.

Take the B flat major fugue in the first book of the
" 48." I venture to think this fugue deserves " practice " as much from the man who means to hear it
as from the man who means to play it to him. It
is just about the most economical piece of music ever
written. The whole thing is made up of three little
tunes—the tightest-fitted little bit of musical mechan-
ism, yet all working so smoothly that it seems like a
living organism rather than a piece of machinery, and
all sounding so spontaneous that you imagine old
Bach threw it off in a spare half-hour whilst waiting
for his breakfast on a sunny morning. A good many
people can carry two tunes in their head at one time
(though not so many as you would think !). But when
Bach gives you these three jolly little tunes all together
in this way :

and then turns them upside down, so that what was
the bottom one becomes the top, and what was the
middle becomes the bottom, and what was the top

becomes the middle, and when he goes on making all his " entries " out of such varied combinations in different keys, and makes even his " episodes " out of scraps of the same three tunes similarly treated— then it is that the uninstructed and untrained listener begins to be a bit bewildered, and if this fugue were not a particularly bright and even jolly one the poor man would plead an engagement elsewhere and leave us to play our musty old fugues to ourselves. And the worst is that Haydn, Mozart, and Beethoven, too, are full of this sort of " science," and however much the unguided listener may get out of their string quartets and symphonies you may be sure he loses quite as much more. Nay, even the popular Wagner is nothing but " counterpoint," and the " Master- singers " overture has a delicious combination of themes (if you can but seize it), which to the naked eye has a remarkable notational resemblance to the two extracts just given.

There is merely one of the little difficulties of the ordinary sort of fellow who likes music but gets lost before it has been going on long—the contrapuntal difficulty. But remember, too, that this fellow when he hears an orchestral piece cannot distinguish a horn passage from a trumpet passage, or an oboe melody from a clarinet melody. So in addition to the intri- cacies of lineal design he has the bewilderments of colour—for if you cannot give a name to a thing you cannot get much of a hold of it, and even in so simple an orchestral piece as a Haydn Symphony not to know what the instruments are about is to lose half the pleasure.

And then, too, there is the difficulty of " periods " and " schools." It is no use looking at an El Greco with a Collier-accustomed eye, or considering a Goya with a Millais-mind. To you and me there are one or two clear chains of development perceptible (a Bach-Haydn-Mozart-Beethoven-Wagner chain, for instance, with a number of plainly defined links and close connections), but for, say, three out of ten of those who do go to concerts (and ten out of ten of those who do not) all composers are merged in one inextricable jumble, and the most that many people can do is to sort them into two heaps that they call by such names as " classical " and " popular," or some others equally foolish.

If there is one thing certain it is that we have got to clear up this and all the other jumbles in the public mind before music can flourish. Not three per cent. of our present population is equipped to enjoy an Elgar symphony. You cannot support A 1 composers on a C 3 population, and " Training—Training—Training ! " must be our cry until things are righted. Fortunately the training has begun. The school teachers are busy, and so are the gramophone makers. And so are other people. But of this I am sure, that until we recognize clearly that people cannot, as things are, be *expected* to appreciate a good concert, so long they never will. It is our business not merely to provide music, but to show people how to enjoy it. You cannot even get the horse to the water at present, for he knows he doesn't know how to drink. We have got to teach him that, and then perhaps he will think it worth while to come.

WILL Wales face the truth ?   Or when the truth reaches it will it always expend its energy in petty protests ?   Potentially the Welsh are one of the most musical nations of the world.   For a proof of that statement look through Dr. Lloyd Williams's collection of Welsh folk-song, or consider the story of the early harmonic development of Wales.   Here is the statement of Giraldus Cambrensis, at the end of the twelfth century :

The Britons do not sing in unison like the inhabitants of other countries, but in many different parts. So that when a company of singers, among the common people, meet to sing, as is usual in this country, as many different parts are heard as there are performers.

But Wales (everybody knows it) has temporarily fallen out of the musical procession.   That it has a wish to rejoin it (perhaps at the head) is clear from many admirable activities.   If it does not once again " fall in " it will be the fault of a little group of people who think it less patriotic to strive after perfection than to pretend they already have it.

" The extraordinarily successful and world-famous —— Male Voice Choir " lately appeared at the Queen's Hall.   " ' Wonderful singing ' (*vide* Press) ; ' It is a

sensation ' ; ' Held the immense audience spellbound ' ;
' Nothing short of marvellous.' '' (I take these un-
attested but doubtless accurately quoted expressions
of admiration from the advance announcement issued
to the public.) I was of the impression that, in choral
singing, at least, Wales still held a certain pre-eminence.
I discounted those adjectives somewhat, but went
honestly expecting great enjoyment, and found a body
of choral singers deficient in several points of choral
technique, and in matters of taste, in choice of programme, and in performance quite beneath contempt.
I am in the habit of saying what I think (a habit
which alone gives any force or value to musical criticism), and on this occasion I did not put myself under
constraint. I take the following rejoinder from the
" Western Mail " :

The comments have aroused resentment in certain
quarters in South Wales, and when the Choir visited
the Mumbles the veteran conductor took the opportunity to make a reply. Members of the audience
expressed the view that Wales should move seriously
in connection with the frequent attacks by English
critics upon Welsh choral effort, some of them even
going so far as to suggest that as a protest Wales
should refuse to have any of the ultra-modern school
as adjudicators at Eisteddfodau, and also that Welsh
musicians should refuse to learn any of their works.

This, I think, is rather childish. There are certain
people who, when a music critic comments unfavour-
ably on their work, will always seek the explanation
in anything but the music. I am not anti-Welsh, nor
do I know any critic who is. Had an English, Scottish,

Irish, Fijian, or Patagonian choir sung such a programme in such a way my comments would have been the same ; and the suggestion that bold little Wales should punish me by boycotting works and workers of the " ultra-modern school " is amusing !

As a matter of well-known fact, my failure to appreciate a good deal of " ultra-modernity " has led to my being, in some quarters, condemned as old-fashioned, my real view being that in forming a critical judgment antiquity is nothing, modernity is nothing, and only quality counts. That the Queen's Hall programme did not please me was due not to its being old-fashioned (which it decidedly was), but to its being, for a great part, cheap and foolish. Here is, of course, a matter of taste. All I can do is to give the programme in full and leave readers, Welsh and English, to judge for themselves :

Introduction : " Hail ! Noble King and Queen."
1. Requiem, " Peace to the Souls " . Caldicott
   Chorus, " Soldiers " (Faust) . . . . Gounod
2. Song, " Baner ein Gwlad " (" The Flag of Our
   Country ") . . . . Dr. Parry
3. National Airs :
   (a) " Annie Laurie " . . . Arr. by Fletcher
   (b) " Killarney " . . . . Arr. by Fletcher
   (c) " Harlech."
   (d) " Home, Sweet Home " . . Arr. Oakley
4. Duet, " Soldiers and Comrades " . . Adlam
5. (a) " Pa-Ma-Lou " . . . . . . S. Powell
   (b) " Old Black Joe."
6. Hymn, " Gotha " (Welsh Hymnal)
                    H.R.H. Albert Prince Consort
7. Song, " I fear no foe " . . . . Pinsuti

8. Chorus, (*a*) " Jolly Roger " . . . Chandish
        (*b*) " Italian Salad " Finale Genée's Opera
9. Song, " Fifinella."
10. Song, " Selected."
11. Welsh Hymn, " Y Delyn Aur " (" The Golden Harp ") . . . . D. Pughe Evans
12. Song, " The Song of all the Ages ". . Squire
13. (*a*) " Martyrs of the Arena " . . . de Rille
   (*b*) " The Long Day Closes ". . . . Sullivan
14. Finale, National Anthem.

As a Queen's Hall programme (" the same programme as at the Royal Command Performance, Windsor Castle, April 18, 1922 ") this is decidedly poor, and it must, further, be explained that the apparently best items in it, the choral settings of national airs, were in reality some of the worst, their " arrangement " being maudlin, and in performance made more so by extremely sentimental singing, at a funereal speed and with a tear-drop on every note.

We may just as well thrash out this Welsh quarrel whilst we are about it. But I hope it is known that fundamentally the quarrel lies not between Welsh musicians and English critics, but between one body of Welsh musical people and another. Events will certainly made this clear shortly, as a similar condition has become clear in the case of the Irish political quarrel. We in England have our interest in it—a natural interest and a kindly one. The issue concerns us, unless we are very parochially-minded Britons. But it concerns Wales much more.

We may, for convenience, call the two parties in Welsh music the Reformers and the Unreformables.

I have received, by letter and by word of mouth, a good many expressions of opinion from both parties. Here is the Reformer attitude, as expressed by a gentleman bearing a name which stamps him as Welsh of the Welsh :

" My object in writing is to express my complete agreement with what you have written about music in Wales. It is very mildly put ; I could wish you had gone further. Wales must be told the whole truth, and Wales has got to stand being told and to face the facts. Not till she does so is there any chance of improvement. There has been a great deal too much fulsome flattery, nay, worse than flattery, lying.

" I went to the National Eisteddfod at Carnarvon last summer, after an interval of many years, and was bitterly disappointed with the music. Wales has gone back fifteen years instead of going forward. My wife, who is an accomplished musician, and who, when we lived in South Wales some sixteen years ago, had ample opportunity of judging Welsh music, agreed with me entirely. ' Potentially,' as you say, ' the Welsh are one of the most musical nations of the world ' ; actually, at the present time, they are one of the most backward.

" As a Welshman I sincerely hope that no stupid protests will prevent you from proclaiming the truth. You are really doing Wales a great service."

So far as possible I want Welshmen themselves to speak, and so absolve me from the charge of jealous foreign interference. I have a Welsh *dossier* in my collection of musico-literary material, and I find amongst its documents the following from a report

of a speech recently made by Mr. E. T. Davies, Director
of Music in the University College of North Wales,
Bangor :

Mr. Davies said that one of the weaknesses of the
Welsh people in the matter of music was a limited
knowledge and narrow horizon, and their limitations
included an appalling ignorance of classical and
instrumental music, of absolute music, independent
of words, music that was a joy in itself, such as chamber
music and orchestral music of all kinds. Their limitations in these respects were pathetic.

The choice of music of their principal institutions
—the Eisteddfod and the Cymanfa Ganu—left much
room for improvement. To be ancient was honourable, but to be unprogressive was foolish, and they
would be astonished if they knew how obstinate
and how determined to stick in the old places many
of the committees who controlled those festivals
were. No finer audience for music could be found
than the average Eisteddfod audience, but he had
often seen them sitting for seven or eight hours listening to stuff the portions of which worth listening to
could have been got through in an hour. That was
a waste of valuable enthusiasm.

It is lack of self-criticism that at present works the
artistic ruin of Wales. And, as already shown, not
only does the Unreformable party refrain from criticism, but it is intolerant of criticism from others. I
am going to entertain you now by the quotation in
full of a letter lately received, but as you read it and
chuckle over its vigorous Old Testament denunciations
of the unrighteous I want you to feel just a little

friendly sympathy, for here is, at any rate, a burning patriotism—though wrongly applied :

" It is high time the critics of foreign names were stopped in this country.

" Their *senselessness* is in keeping with their *meanness*, and, as the Indians say, ' Stinginess comes to grief ! '

" The public must rise up in a body and thrash them—intellectually !

" They are to be seen in public halls, and are known from their presuming bad manners, and the trash they write is in keeping with their lack of good breeding.

" They are a *deadly influence*, and the public will settle them, and *deal with them*.

" Our national music (Welsh choirs and others) will not be torn to shreds by these dyspeptic minds.

" And may it ' come home ' to them, 10,000 times and all their families.

" May all they do and say be as futile as their merciless and inhuman criticisms.

" To slay our true British art is infamous, and these critics are the Devil's own.

" May they never prosper, for all the mischief they do to the defenceless, the widow and the fatherless, and struggling genius.

" From one who knows the *true music* of descendants of Llewellyn the Great and last Prince of Wales !

" May God punish these unjust critics for staying His spiritually conveyed art and music.

" Let them live to beg their bread ! "

This is a real Imprecatory Psalm, and I can imagine that many pious and patriotic Welsh Church households will welcome its appearance here and, gathering round the family harmonium, sing it to an Anglican chant ; I have myself tried it to Jones in D minor, and it goes stirringly.

And now, having as much as possible in the latter part of this essay left Welshmen themselves to discuss their music, I beg to be allowed, for once, to turn to a purely personal question. The insinuation about myself, when often repeated (and I hear it pretty often), becomes a bit of a bore, so, though I must admit that my family is foreign, I want to say, once and for all, that we have been naturalized for some little time. The word " Scholes " has become a common enough English place-name, as may be seen by reference to the Post Office Directory. We came over with our fellow-Danes, in the reign of Egbert, a thousand years ago. On the distaff side I have an older heritage in the country—coming of the same stock as that of all the writers here quoted, including, I regret to say, the rude one.

A FEW SUGGESTIONS UPON POPULAR MUSIC

I. " DOPE " [1]

ONE of the many recent communications received on the subject of the popular appreciation of music deals with a case of conscience. Its writer is a lover of " the creations of great men " ; as a measure of the effect they have upon him he tells me that he actually " prefers to listen to them in silence." But this ardent spirit also loves to express itself in the dance. " Not to dance, be it understood, in the manner of M. Novikof or M. Volinine or M. Diaghilef, perhaps [I didn't know Diaghilef danced, but he may !], but to dance with the young ladies of my acquaintance in an orderly and well-behaved manner. [A reflection here, you note, on Messrs. N., V. and D.] But then comes the difficulty : what music is one to dance to ? " The " Great Men," this reader tells me, do not write dance music, and their neglect, combined with the decadent dancing customs of the day, drives him to " Jazz " :

" Tell me, am I living a Jekyll-and-Hyde existence, in thus openly avowing a taste for *Music* whilst in secret I must all too frequently suborn wicked fellows

[1] " Do you look upon Music as ' Dope '—a drugging sensuality ? " (A writer in the " Daily Express.")

66

to play me Jazz ?   Or is it permissible for an ' Ordinary Dancer ' to view ' Jazz ' merely as an accessory
to a purely physical enjoyment, and to look upon
the strains of the coloured minstrels as passing directly
from his ears to his feet, leaving his musical senses
untouched and unoffended ? "

Now who am I that I should be constituted this
reader's father confessor ?   But I admit his predica-
ment, and the fault I feel lies not so much with him
as with the " Great Men." Past history has proved
that it is not impossible to write music that will
provide at one and the same time for the pleasures
of the toes and of the ears, and if this reader but had
justice at the hands of our present-day composers and
publishers, the carnal and spiritual sides of his highly
strung temperament would in the ball-room receive
equal satisfaction.   His dangerous double life should
be unnecessary. Tell me, do any of our musical
" Great Men " themselves dance, and if so to what
music do they do so ?   Our serious professional musical
body, the Incorporated Society of Musicians, used at
its annual conference to refresh itself after each day's
toil by an evening in the ball-room.   Did it do so at
that conference at which Sir Hugh Allen denounced
" Beastly Tunes " ?   And if so, to what did it dance ?
An answer to that question might help us.

But the two letters that interest me most are
respectively from the lady who teaches music to the
blinded soldiers at St. Dunstan's and a young amateur
composer.   The lady wins my respect in two ways.
She has had the good sense to go through the academic
mill, and she has had the strength to come out of it

open-minded. In order that I may understand the view of music she is by training likely to adopt in her work she tells me that she is a Licentiate of the Royal Academy of Music, of which she was for four years a student, and that she was a pupil of the learned Professor Ebenezer Prout. But at St. Dunstan's this academically accomplished musician is trying to teach the piano pupils " what they like," which, provided she also tries to extend their " likings " in all sorts of desirable directions, is admirable. She says, " I usually get the tunes first-hand from the men, who go about a good deal to music halls, etc.," and adds :

" I find that the popular airs which appeal to them are the best ones of what they hear : the ' rubbish ' they will have nothing to do with, *so that our tunes are few in number.* As so much so-called popular music is published it is just as well to note how much of it is rejected by the untaught ear of a musical man who judges and chooses only by his ear without association of any other sort."

That, I think, is rather striking confirmation of the assertion I have made that people do not demand bad music—though they may often have bad music thrust upon them and accept it without protest. These very St. Dunstan's pianists, I should imagine, may applaud any sort of a bright tune at the music hall, but that is not to say they are entirely without a sense of values, and when it comes to deciding which tunes are worth the labour of learning, without eyes, at the piano the critical spirit asserts itself.

As for the amateur composer, he asks me a question

that I knew I had let myself in for, and was sure
somebody would spring upon me—" Don't you think
you might follow up your discussion of ' good ' and
' bad ' tunes by telling us *what is a good tune ?* "

Frankly, I am not quite sure that I can. Has anyone yet successfully defined " good " and " bad " in
poetry or pictures ? But I have long had it in my
mind to try, and from time to time have jotted down,
as they occurred to me, candidates for admission to
a list of " The World's Best Twenty Tunes," or something of the sort—the great tunes, like the " London-
derry Air," and "Che faro," and the "Old Hundredth."
That seems to me to be the only way to get at the
principles of "goodness"—to examine actual fine
specimens and discover the secret of their qualities.
Perhaps some one has already done this, but, if so,
I do not recall it. Meantime there is one thing I
can do. I can give a rule which will enable our young
friend to detect and condemn an enormous proportion
of the " bad " tunes, and so to avoid wasting time over
them. The rule is simply this : Whatever tune tries
to " get at " your cheaper emotions is " bad." It is
a simple test, but few think of applying it. You see
the trick often in religion. A very thoughtful Baptist
minister complained bitterly to me a few years ago
about some of his colleagues who had won a danger-
ously great following by thumping the Bible and
crying, " The Blood, brethren, the *Blood*, the BLOOD ! "
In some Anglican churches the same appeal is made
by the words of the weaker specimens in " Hymns
Ancient and Modern," and in some continental Catholic
churches by tawdry decoration and trivial art—what

a more serious and cultured French Catholic would speak of, with a kindly smile, as mere " *Bon-dieuserie.*"

As my friend, Mr. Darewski, has been active in discussing this question of " good " and " bad," I am going to take an example from a batch of pieces he recently sent me for review, but, in fairness, I would say that his publications are no worse than those of many others, and that there are probably not more than three or four publishers in the country (if that number !) whose music is entirely free from this attempt to " get at " our soft side, though some of them demand from their composers a higher standard of workmanship than others. (As a matter of fact, the very respectable publishers of church music are amongst the very worst of the offenders.) Here, then, is the opening " symphony " of a song from the batch :

There is the very rant of false pathos. The thing

is not "true," and if only people would reflect a moment they would resent it as they resent the whine of a street beggar. In looking at this example you will see at once that the false appeal is made chiefly through sentimentalized harmony, and the interesting point arises whether this is not always the case, and whether, after all, a melody (*qua* melody, and apart from any harmonic implication it may cunningly embody) can really succeed in being vulgar ? If so, there are no bad "tunes" in the strictest sense of the word "tune." At all events, it occurs to me that it is very difficult to be vulgar (as distinct from merely commonplace or clumsy) when dealing in melody alone.

II. SOME "SERIOUS CRITICISM"

I have a niece who has, I am sorry to say, been leading a rather godless life. Indeed, for four years she had not so much as set foot in any place of Christian worship, until, a few Sundays ago, moved by the entreaties of some who had her welfare much at heart, she consented to go to Church. Her memories of the ritual were vague. She had difficulty in finding her place in the Prayer Book. Until her attention was called to her error she even held it upside down. And when the solemn organ played, and the white-robed choir stood up in their carven stalls, she amazed her more reverent fellow-worshippers by inquiring in a clear soprano voice—"*Mummy, are they going to sing 'Bubbles' ?*" Mr. Francis Clarke, who wrote a long article in "The London Mercury," and a letter

(almost as long) in the " Observer," might well ask,
" Do the critics really know the popular music ? "
I confess to him that until in serious family conclave
that disturbing incident was discussed I had never
so much as heard of " Bubbles." But at Mr. Clarke's
suggestion (for he accepted an offer I made him, and
sent me his list of the six popular songs I am to submit
to " serious criticism ") I have bought a copy and—
I must talk to that child's parents !

" Bubbles " (or, in full, " I'm For Ever Blowing
Bubbles ") I found to be a mere two pages long,
and it cost two shillings. It's superiority to Beethoven is thus manifest. No publisher dare charge
you a shilling a page for Beethoven ; you can get
his thirty-two Sonatas, running to over 400 pages,
for about 8s. 6d., which works out at a mere half-
penny per two pages. " Bubbles " is " Sung by Fred
Barnes." His portrait, with a very good set of
teeth and a nice pipe, appeared on the cover in large
letters, and in much smaller letters we were told that
the work was " Written and Composed by John
Kenbrovin and John William Kellette." I like this
spirit of co-partnership—two poets and two composers, I suppose (to use a technical musical term,
" four-in-two "), neither of whom desires our exclusive
admiration for either poem or music. It suggests a
true fusion of the arts—not the poem first coming
into existence and then being tamely " set " to music,
but the two born together with an enduring Siamese
bond. And yet, carefully studying " Bubbles," I
almost begin to wonder whether the old-fashioned
Purcellian, Schubertian, Schumannesque, Wolfian,

Elgarian system of setting lyric genius to work was not in some ways better. This bold, modern plan seems somehow to work rather unfairly to nouns and verbs, and much too generously to conjunctions and prepositions and unimportant adverbs and pronouns. Here is some of the accentuation of one verse:

" *When* shadows creep, *when* I'm asleep,
    To lands of hope I stray,
  Then at day-*break*, *when* I awake,
    My blue bird flutters away."

But this is perhaps hyper-criticism! It may even be asked, and with some justice, " Who listens to the words of a song ? " I pass then to the music itself, turning first to the chorus, for in this form of musical art the chorus is in effect the song, and the song a mere prelude-to-a-chorus. I somehow miss the touch of originality in this chorus. I suppose I am *blasé*, for I seem to have heard something like its melody years ago. Dare I say that those familiar phrases never really thrilled me, and now strike me as almost commonplace ? That Peggy should enjoy it is against Wordsworthian theory, for a being who but four short years ago descended to this earth, trailing clouds of glory and with the far-off echoes of heavenly harps still ringing in her pink baby ears, should surely retain some sort of a musical standard. Either Wordsworth is wrong or else Heaven is not the sort of place we have always been told, and certainly no place for a music critic—to which last suggestion Mr. Fred Barnes, Mr. John Kenbrovin, Mr. John William Kellette, Mr. Hermann Darewski, and Mr. Francis Clarke will probably add confirmatory opinions.

Now for the song itself, the prelude-verse as distinct from the chorus. Its harmonies are open to discussion. Personally, I do not quite like these sevenths and ninths on the strong beat of the bar. Try them on your piano and see how you, on your part, feel about them :

It may be old-fashioned of me, but though I admit I can quite well stand that sort of thing in Holst's "Planets," for some reason it jars on me in a simple song. Then, melodically and harmonically, I myself feel the following to be, shall I say, a trifle meagre in effect. Economy of notes has here, I fear, gone too far :

Mr. Clarke in his article was downright and scathing —" It would be best, of course, if Sir Hugh Allen and Mr. Scholes would compose good popular music instead of abusing the bad." Really I think we must try. I must mention it to Sir Hugh. If we were to put our heads together, as Mr. Kenbrovin and Mr. Kellette have done, I think we might produce some " Bubbles." And if we could but inflate them with the wind of the combined commercial enterprise of the " Kendis-Brockman Music Co., Inc.," " Jerome H. Remick and Co., New York and Detroit," and Messrs. Feldman and Co., of New Oxford Street, I do not see why our " Bubbles," too, should not sail away over the continents without bursting. But I must approach Sir Hugh tactfully. He has, I gather from Mr. Clarke, come to be looked upon as a man of strong speech, and if I were to spring that proposition on him incautiously he might hastily reply (and not in the sense I want)—" Bubbles be Blowed ! "

Much more instinctive musical ability and solid workmanship have gone to the making of " Swanee," another of the songs I am asked seriously to criticize, than to that of " Bubbles." " Swanee " has rhythm, and its formal construction is very skilful. Its harmonies, too, however much you may dislike some of them, are, at least the work of a man who knows what he is about, whereas the harmonies of " Bubbles " strike one as the incompetent work of a hand that does not even know how to achieve vigorous vulgarity. Moreover, the words of " Bubbles " merely toy with a pretty sentiment, whereas those of " Swanee " get down to something instinctive, elemental, primal— namely, that powerful longing which the population of the British Isles has for some years past felt to be united to its native " Dixie," to fall again into the arms of its " Mam," who is " waiting and praying " for its return. The appeal of the words of " Swanee " is enhanced by a happy device : at a point indicated in the score the vocalist to whom its interpretation is entrusted lapses momentarily into the spoken voice. The words so treated are touching. In simple, direct phrase they imagine the exaltation of the wanderer re-united to his beloved South-land home—" I'll be happy ! I'll be happy ! " he cries.

This pathetic exclamation, as will be observed, is daringly accompanied on the piano or orchestra by nine simple, but rhythmic, repetitions of the note C natural, strikingly recalling a similar touch of symbolism in Browning :

I feel for the common chord again,
Sliding by semitones, till I sink to the minor,—yes,
And I blunt it to a ninth, and I stand on alien ground,
Surveying awhile the heights I rolled from into the
    deep ;
Which, hark, I have dared and done, for my resting-
    place is found,
The C Major of this life ; so, now I will try to sleep.

Browning's " sliding by semitones " is, by the way,

a characteristic of both the songs at present under review :

FROM "BUBBLES."

FROM "SWANEE."

But this attractive characteristic is not confined to Messrs. Vogler, Kenbrovin, Kellette, and Gershwin ; Spohr, Barnby and others of our severest modern ecclesiastical composers have used it in many moving passages of their church music.

It should be mentioned that the words of " Swanee " are given as by " I. Cæsar," which carries their composition back, one imagines, to the campaign of 55 B.C. It may be guessed, however, that some modern hand has given the poem its happy present-day touches, reproducing with great subtlety and appropriateness the Roman general's longing for his southern home under the paraphrase of " Swanee, how I love you ! how I love you ! " The imperial poet goes on, " My dear old Swanee, I would give the world . . . ," and in that last phrase we see the

steady, patriotic purpose behind the Roman legion-
aries' dreams of universal conquest. I call special
attention to this element of historical interest, as it
is one which may possibly have escaped Mr. Clarke
and his friends of the music-halls.

In my next essay I propose to apply myself to
serious criticism of two more of the songs mentioned
by Mr. Clarke in the very kind letter he has sent me—
" I Passed by Your Window " and " Come to the
Fair."

III.   More " Serious Criticism "

Passing, in response to Mr. Clarke's demand, that
" music critics should tell the people exactly what
they like and dislike and why," to two more of the
popular songs on his list, I *like* " I Passed by Your
Window " and " Come to the Fair," because both
have simple, attractive melodies, such as anyone at
a first hearing can enjoy, and also simple, harmless
words (a great point, the latter, seeing that the words
of many popular songs suggest that they have been
written by nursemaids for nursemaids). And I
dislike them because they both have badly managed,
commonplace accompaniments. I must justify this
by examples, I suppose.

(1) Miss Brahe in her " Window " has but three
harmonic panes. Practically the whole tune, in
both verses, is economically harmonized out of the
three primary chords (Tonic, Dominant, and Sub-
dominant—Doh, Soh, Fah). This in itself does not
condemn her ; Chopin's whole long " Berceuse " has
only two chords. But, in the case of the " Window,"

in the second half of each verse, those chords are clumsily managed ; I cannot spare space to reproduce the passage, but let readers who still have the song play it over, *really listening* to the effect (most lovers of popular song, I gather, do not listen to the accompaniments), and they will recognize what I mean when I say that any elementary harmony pupil, in, say, his second month of study, might write such a bass as that, and get it heavily blue-pencilled for his pains —or lack of them.

(2) Mr. Easthope Martin, in " Come to the Fair," begins thus :

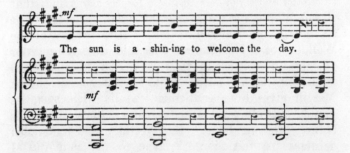

The sun is a - shin-ing to welcome the day.

There, in the very second bar, the composer has gone out of his key. Nothing necessarily wrong about that ! Beethoven, in his First Symphony, actually began with his first chord out of the key. But an effect like this should be sparingly used, and Mr. Martin repeats that same modulatory progression at least four times in every one of his verses, i.e., twelve times in all. Would the " people " have enjoyed this song less if the composer had put into its accompaniment a little more of the art he shows

in others of his compositions—for Mr. Easthope
Martin has the reputation of being one of the most
refined of our more " popular " composers ?

Now as to originality ! I do not think we must
ask for too much of it in a " popular " composer.
Originality is the rarest quality in art, and this sort
of music is admittedly journalism rather than literature.
Let us, then, be satisfied if we get an article of good
quality, and not pry too closely into its origins. But
if we were to begin to pry, we should not find much
that is really new in either of these pleasant melodies.
Mr. Clarke has told us that " *a new tune will always
be rightly more popular, because for its own generation
it will always have a greater spiritual value than an
old tune of equal absolute merit.*" And the great Mr.
Walkley, of " The Times," has said that the efforts
of certain musicians to revive folk-tunes always
strike him as a " forlorn hope." But Mr. Easthope
Martin gives both gentlemen the lie. His song is
popular, yet old, Mr. Clarke ! It shows that " revival "
is no " forlorn hope," Mr. Walkley ! For if not
actually " a folk-tune," " Come to the Fair " is a
cento of favourite bits of folk-tune. The first phrase,
for instance, is of a type common enough in our
folk-songs. You get it pretty exactly in " The
Cuckoo's Nest."

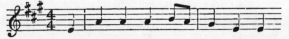

The next phrase (Heigh ho, Come to the Fair),
and the way in which it is introduced as a sort of
refrain, suggest indebtedness to some sea chantey :

taking up the first volume of chanties to hand, on
its first page I find not quite the very notes, it is true,
but the very same musical idea, introduced in the
same way (the chorus phrase of " Mudder Dinah "—
" Sing ! Sally oh ! Right fol-de-ray "). After this Mr.
Martin repeats his " Cuckoo " phrase, and passes to
a long quotation from the good old tune, " When
Johnny comes Marching Home." By and by we get
our " Cuckoo " and our chantey again, and so ends
the verse. I am not grumbling. I even welcome
the case as an argument against the unrevivability
of folk-song amongst " the people." There is a fortune
in folk-songs ! Let some of these astute publishers
put behind folk-tune anything approaching the amazing commercial " push and go " they put behind their
present " popular songs," and I believe they will
prove Mr. Walkley no prophet.

Exaggerating but slightly, I may say that I enjoyed
" I Passed by Your Window " long before Miss Brahe
composed it. Under the title of " Batiste's Famous
Andante in F," it once had probably the largest
sale of any organ piece ever published, and was
familiar to every worshipper of any denomination
that made use of the organ. I have only space here
for a parallel exhibition of the mere opening phrases
of the two pieces :

And now, if Mr. Clarke will excuse me, I will leave
my "serious criticism." The remaining pieces on
his list are published by a firm of publishers of whom
he himself, in a very kind letter to me, makes admis-
sions. He called on them, he says, to see what they
had that was new and popular and was shown only
"some dreary stuff by Mr. ——." He adds, "I
doubt whether there is enough dullness in the country
to fulfil Messrs. ——'s expectations of these songs."
But stay! Here is Mr. Clarke himself forgetting
that one's duty is to "compose good popular music
instead of abusing the bad." Let him get to work!

IV.   QUALITY IN MUSIC

It is often a surprise to me to discover how remote
from the minds of many music-lovers is the idea of
a definite basis for critical opinion, in the existence of
good or bad "quality" in music, the word being used
almost in the sense in which a cloth-merchant or
cabinet-maker might use it. Any one of my readers
could say in a moment what is wrong with the style
of such a passage as this (from "A Literal Translation
of the New Testament," by Rev. Edmund Harwood,
D.D., 1768) :

"The servant said, 'Your brother, Sir, is just
returned from abroad, and your father is celebrating
this happy occasion by a most splendid and elegant
entertainment.'"

But when we turn from literature to music few people
seem to have any definite grounds for their opinions.

Let me give a very simple example of what I mean
by bad musical " quality."   It was recently advertised
in the Press that at the Albert Hall Dame Clara Butt
would sing a new song, of which a portion was given
with the suggestion, " Try over this refrain " :

I should have thought that to any musical person
whatever, however untrained, that melody would be
very irritating. A somewhat undistinguished phrase
is, first, enunciated ; then, lifted two notes higher
(with its quasi-syncopation intact and already becoming tiresome) ; third, lifted still two notes higher
(one very tiny change being introduced at the end) ;
and fourth, allowed to drop to its original position,
and then given out once more (I hope finally, but
cannot say, as the so proudly displayed extract goes
no further). The passage as a whole is, of course,
to say the least, an abuse of the technical device of
" sequence."   The personality and the voice of the
distinguished singer engaged to produce the song
may have " carried it across " and obtained for it
a few months' vogue, and the lilt may, I suppose,

in itself, have been temporarily attractive to simple musical minds, but, with the greatest confidence, I defy such a melody to achieve even the moderate allowance of five years' life—and the collective sense of the community, spread over a lengthened period, is the final justification or refutation of the more immediate opinions of the professional critic.

Now it is not that this tune is too simple. That immortal theme of Beethoven at the end of the Choral Symphony is just as much so:

But the one tune has "quality" and the other, decidedly, has not. Beethoven might conceivably (though not, I think, probably) have begun a tune with just that same first bar-and-a-half as Mr. Ivor Novello, but he would have made much more of it, and, though even he, like all composers, had his less careful moments, he would certainly somewhere in its course have provided a point of greatest emotion, as we may call it, such as is here entirely wanting (note in the Choral Symphony example the strong effect of the drop to the low A, once, and once only, introduced).

This misuse of the easy device of sequence is merely

one example of melodic bad quality. Another very frequent lapse in melodic craftsmanship is carelessness at the points of cadence. I cite Sullivan somewhat falteringly, for, though I am avowedly one of the warmest admirers of his genius, I no sooner get a word or two of measured judgment off my pen than I receive letters of violent abuse. I suggest to those who love Sullivan not wisely but too well, that they take any chance dozen of his melodies and examine the lines preceding what we may call the middle comma and the final full stop. I believe they will be surprised to find how frequently Sullivan, having begun well, falls, when approaching a period, into the merest fill-up-the-line commonplace. The fact that this is so rarely detected suggests to me that psychologically the cadence passage of a tune is the least important, yet a fine composer will not, on that account, neglect it, nor will a careful listener consent at that point to have something conventional fobbed off on him.

The details which combine to make up " quality " in melody are, however, too many for discussion here. General curve, position of highest and lowest notes, rhythm, skilful " development " of longer passages from some simple germ, are all to be looked into. Though nobody will ever get quite to the bottom of its mysteries, to some extent the subject of quality in melody has been studied. See, for instance, Parry's admirable " Style in Musical Art," Stanford's " Musical Composition," Combarieu's " Music, its Laws and Evolution," and the brief article " Melody " in Grove's Dictionary. And hear,

as a popular exposition, the set of " Melody Lectures "
prepared by Sir Walford Davies, and recently issued
as records by the Gramophone Co. Better still,
write down the six or twelve melodies you think the
best in the world (see page 69) and try if you can find
in what lies their appeal (in other words, what constitutes their supreme " quality "), and, on the other
hand, take six melodies that you feel to be poor and
study the causes of their evident lack of " quality."
And, having done this, begin to study " quality "
in harmony, in the " form," or laying out, of a piece,
in adaptation of means to ends by the choice of the
right sort of passage for the instrument written for,
in the manner of combination of instruments (in an
orchestral piece), and so forth. Cultivate an ear for
good " style " and bad " style," and, at last, find
yourself as ready to detect clumsiness, sentimentality,
or bombast in music as you are in literature. You
will, of course, sometimes be wrong, as the most
experienced and thoughtful music critics sometimes
are, but, at all events, you will be wrong with a reason,
and hence more ready to put yourself right.

A FEW REMARKS ON OPERA

I. The Pace of Opera

A GENTLEMAN has lately written to me offering me a fee if I will read an opera libretto he has written and give him my opinion upon it. And I have refused, because my views upon opera libretti are so heterodox that anyone who paid me a fee for a personal application of them would be sure to want his money back. To begin with, I share Beethoven's objection—there is far too much murder and adultery about opera libretti. A good exciting crime is all very well in its way, but opera libretti in general seem to be written for the class of people for whom the recent Thompson-Bywaters hanging was providentially followed by the mystery of the locked-up tailor and the body in the bath. This, however, is a minor objection. Wickedness one can stand, but boredom never, and the normal opera libretto is surely tedious beyond expression. It moves so slowly, the fault to some extent being that librettists do not sufficiently distinguish themselves from playwrights, forgetting that what in a spoken play would pass over in a few seconds will be prolonged, once it gets into the hands of a composer, into as many minutes or more.

Of all the slow-paced opera-writers Wagner is, of

course, the slowest. His libretti, read as plays, though too long and involved, do not come out badly ; it is the setting to music that makes them so tiresome. It has become so usual to take out large slices of Wagner's music and give it in concert performance that I almost wonder nobody has tried the other thing—to take out the words and give them without the music. There is many a passage that one thinks rather fine when one reads it before going to the opera-house which yet becomes insufferable when it is drawled out to a copious orchestral commentary. Vernon Lee gets to the point, I think, in her account of her first visit to Bayreuth (in a letter to Maurice Baring quoted in his recent " The Puppet Show of Memory ") :

Surely all great art of every sort has a certain coyness which makes it give itself always less than wanted ; look at Mozart ; he will give you a whole act of varying dramatic expression (think of the first act of " Don Giovanni ") of deepest, briefest pathos and swift humour, a dozen perfect songs or concerted pieces, in the time it takes for that old *poseur*, Amfortas, to squirm over his Grail, or Kundry to break the ice with Parsifal. Even " Tristan," so incomparably finer than Wagner's other things, is indecent through its dragging out of situations, its bellowing out of confessions which the natural human being dreads to profane by showing or expressing. With all this goes what to me is the chief psychological explanation of Wagner (and of his hypnotic power over some persons), his *extreme slowness of vital tempo*. Listening to him is like finding oneself in a planet where the Time's unit is bigger than ours ; one is on the stretch, devitalized as by the contemplation of a slug.

I feel sure that this passage must be sympathetically received by many who have lately listened to " Siegfried," " The Valkyries " or " The Dusk of the Gods." To go into Covent Garden at 6.30 and come out at 11.30 reflecting on the small amount of "business done," is to feel considerable resentment against the slow-moving Wagner. I do not profess thoroughly to understand the complex psychology of the opera-goer, but I should guess that in " Siegfried " a good many people patiently endure such things as the long speeches of Wotan, and the pointless interpolation of what my friend Mr. Edwin Evans calls the " Potash and Perlmutter Duet " (Alberich and Mime, just after the killing of the dragon), merely in order to be present at the high moments, the Sword Song, the Wood Music, the Fire Music, and the Brünnhilde Awakening. As a matter of fact, a great deal of Wagner must, I feel, be unintelligible to any who have not engaged in earnest preliminary study. Can any reader tell me, for instance, that, from mere attendance at Covent Garden, he came to understand the argument of Wotan to Brünnhilde in the second act of " The Valkyries " ?

Of course, sooner or later we shall have to come to " potted Wagner." There are abridgments already. Our British National Opera Company cuts out a chunk here and there, and hopes we shall never notice such a peculiar proceeding as Wotan announcing three questions and then asking only one. But these clumsy cuts are not enough. A practical " acting edition " of Wagner is necessary—one which will allow us to enter the theatre at eight and leave at eleven. Of course, the whole-length authentic text must occasionally be performed, but the short text, authoritatively arrived at after careful study by a master musician, should be the normal thing.

I come now to a model libretto. It is by Leigh Hunt, and will be found in the definitive edition of his poetical works, just issued under the editorship of its publisher, Mr. Humphrey Milford, of the Oxford University Press. Leigh Hunt knew not Wagner, I should guess, or at any rate knew very little of him (though " Tristan " was finished in the year of Hunt's death). But there were opera-writers before Wagner, and Hunt, in 1830, when Wagner was but seventeen, gave them a lesson from which I fear they did not profit :

THE ESSENCE OF OPERA; OR, ALMANZOR
AND IMOGEN

AN OPERA IN THREE ACTS

ACT I.

Imogen. My love !
Almanzor. My soul !
Both.　　　　At length then we unite !
　　　　People, sing, dance, and show us your delight.
Chorus. Let's sing and dance, and show 'em our delight.

ACT II.

Imogen. O love !
　　　　[*A noise of war.* THE PRINCE *appears, pursued by his enemies. Combat.* THE PRINCESS *faints.* THE PRINCE *is mortally wounded.*]

Almanzor. Alas !
Imogen.   Ah what !
Almanzor.   I die !
Imogen.   Ah me !
          People, sing, dance, and show your misery.
Chorus. Let's sing and dance, and show our misery.

ACT III.

          [PALLAS *descends in a cloud to* ALMAN-
          ZOR, *and speaks.*]
Pallas. Almanzor, live !
Imogen.   Oh bliss !
Almanzor.   What do I see ?
Trio. People, sing, dance, and hail this prodigy.
Chorus. Let's sing and dance, and hail this prodigy.
Now who will set to music that marvel of concision
and completeness ? Of course, he would include an
Overture, and would set the Prologue (which I have
omitted), and, as will be noted, he would have to
provide three Ballets.

II. OPERATIC IMPROBABILITIES

A puzzled philosopher has somewhere remarked
that there are some things no fellow can understand.
Amongst these is surely the fact that on the opera
stage the little simple things are so often badly done.
Let us look first at " The Valkyries," at some
recent performances. I am not unwilling to believe
Wagner's tale of a log hut built around the trunk of a
tree, but I am sceptical of a tree continuing to bear
leaves *inside the hut*. It is true that by an economy of
resource, perhaps justified in the case of an institution

that supplies Wagner music drama at eightpence a seat (including tax), this same tree has to appear later flourishing in the open upon the Valkyries' mountain gathering-ground, but begin its leafy branches a little higher, or, by some ingenuity of stage craft, make the lower branches detachable, and credulity is subjected to a smaller strain.

Another curiosity of nature is seen upon that same Valkyrie mountain. The scene is one in which various characters, overcome by powerful emotions, take it in turns to faint. A soft spot to faint on is, in all humanity, an obvious necessity, and this is provided in the shape of a little rectangular lawn, occurring most unexpectedly in the middle of the rocky mountain summit. Why not cut the edge of the plot a little irregularly, and turn a palpable hearth-rug into plausible herbage?

Speaking of fainting, it is, by the way, a question whether some of the distressing tendency could not be avoided by a little more generosity in the first act ; stage provisions do not cost much, and characters whose operatic duties require them to sing during supper cannot consume large rations. Why, then, should Hunding and Siegelinde, and their guest, Siegmund, sit down to supper at a board bare of all vestige of victual ? " Set the meal now before us," says Hunding, and he is hardly the man to stand trifling ! I look for some protest on his part at a later performance.

The presence of well-cut steps on all rocky places of stage mountains, however remote from existing civilizations, is a phenomenon that might well engage the attention of archæologists—but not of audiences, from whom they might surely be easily hidden by a nice adjustment of masses. (My ingenious typist has here, I note, substituted " mosse___ ___ the suggestion is not impracticable.) Some cr___ ___ ____ power of music may, however, perhaps b___ ___ ___hen we find trees and rocks behaving un___ ___ y, and what would be inadmissible in the r___ ___ en drama may be taken in opera as an ack___ ___ent of the presence of Orpheus, whose p___ ___ ___ such things is admitted.

Talking of Orpheus rem___ ___ of lutes, and that brings me to the genera___ ___ of musical instruments on the operatic st___ ___ re is a lute in " The Mastersingers," and it ___ ___ ___e only stage musical instrument well playe___ ___ ___t Garden at the present time. The soun___ ___ike that of a concealed harp with a strip of ___ ___r threaded through the strings, but it is qui___ ___, and Beckmesser usually suits the action to ___ ___ a life-like way. Moreover, he plays somethi___ ___oks very like a real lute, whereas some s___ ___ists play instruments of as nondescript a ___ ___n as that of F.C.G. in his recent " West___ ___azette " cartoon, where Lady Bonham Cart___ ___del, is shown about to perform to Mr. Asqu___ ___ng Richard, on a sort of bowless fiddle unk___ ___musical antiquarians under any name wha___

The w___ ___ horn in " The Mastersingers " is also not___ ___ne ; its sound suggests a euphonium behind ___ ___s, and the only opportunity for carping critici___ ___ is its wonderful power, when heard played in the distance by one tottering old watchman, to disperse surging crowds of boisterous, able-bodied citizens. There is a quality about that horn that should make it of interest to the representatives of law and order in several centres of population at the present moment.

But if the lutanist in " The Mastersingers " is good, the harpists in " Tannhäuser " are very bad indeed. There is, of course, a considerable body of them. They are, we may take it, the cream of their profession, or they would not be admitted to the Wartburg and District Musical Competition Festival. But they are not even in agreement as to the proper way to hold a harp. Some play with the curved side to the body and others with the straight side, and at one time we actually have a duet with the two performers holding their instruments in different ways. Tannhäuser himself (but, then, he is a very impulsive man and irregular in many of his ways) sometimes holds the harp flat and draws his fingers from treble to bass —producing by this means scales and arpeggios that run from bass to treble !

The shepherd boy in " Tannhäuser " is a skilful performer on the pipe, and so charmingly feminine in his appearance that I could willingly forbear criticism from motives of gallantry ; moreover, this wind instrumentalist is so determined to be life-like that upon one occasion I actually saw him take advantage of a few bars' rest to empty imaginary saliva. But it has worried me once or twice to hear his well-played notes proceeding from his instrument a bar or so before he has placed it to his lips. It is, indeed,

an almost universal failing in stage musicians not to
begin and end with the sound, and to omit to make
their playing movements in the same rhythm as the
notes we hear.

This leads me to recall a case where musicianship
perhaps overshoots itself. Agnes Nicholls, as the
Countess Rosina in " Figaro," reads, apparently, so
well at sight, that when accompanying upon the harp
Cherubino's newly-composed love-song, she is able,
after a mere glance or two at her copy, to look no
more at it, being compelled to let her affectionate eyes
rest henceforth upon the singer. Would that such
fluent sight-playing were more common amongst our
amateur accompanists !

To return to " Tannhäuser " : those state trumpeters
are magnificent, but if I were in a fault-finding mood
(which Heaven forbid !), I would inquire whether
twelfth-century bandsmen bore their music clipped
to their instruments in front of their noses, like the
Salvation Army players of to-day. Before leaving
the trumpeters, let me pay a just tribute to their
leader, who, at a performance not long ago, seeing
a sudden danger of a repetition of the catastrophe
which in similar musical circumstances overtook the
walls of Jericho, had the presence of mind and the
muscular strength to seize and support a group of
three massive Romanesque pillars whilst not merely
playing his own part, but also directing the performance of his fellows. How near to disaster we came
that evening I fancy very few observed.

III. Opera as Seen by an Actor

How would our National Opera Company's staging
and acting strike an actor of the spoken drama ? was
a question I lately asked. I had Wagner more especially in my mind, for in him the difficulties, in both
staging and acting, are at their height. I have now
made a test with the less difficult Charpentier. Looking around lately amongst my friends, I found a
very experienced actor and actress, then taking holiday after an American tour, and, without revealing
my purpose, invited them to join me in my box,
and then listened to their unsuspecting comments.
Neither of them had seen " Louise " before, but I
innocently lent them the libretto in advance, and,
by their intelligent comments to one another, quickly
saw that they had studied it closely from a professional
point of view. I hope my friends will, in a good cause,
pardon the unexpected publicity given to their expert
opinions.

The warmest praise throughout the evening was
given to Miss Licette as " Louise." My friends were,
I think, ignorant of Charpentier's chamber on Montmartre, of his close and sympathetic study of the life
of " the people," and of his social-musical work amongst
working girls; but they were struck with the truth
of his representation of a working-class home, and
very much so with Miss Licette's human treatment of
the daughter of such a home. Again and again they
exclaimed upon the charmingly natural way in which
this impersonation was given.

Mr. Walter Hyde, as Julian, they also admired, but

less. Charpentier (he was, of course, his own librettist) has surely attempted to draw a character a little less stable and serious than Mr. Hyde gives us. Here is a young man who, it is hinted, has had previous love adventures, and who, we are entitled to guess, may even have still others before he dies. A somewhat more evident touch of the scapegrace seems to be called for.

On Mr. Radford's sensitive acting I only caught one adverse comment ; this was during what I always think of as " The Scene of the Soup," since for some minutes the whole family does nothing but sit at its evening meal, gloomily emptying its plates to slow, soft music. After the meal father and daughter are left alone, and modern youthful independence is in conflict with old-style authority. " I wish he'd keep still sometimes, just for a moment," was the remark. " He's moving his arms, his legs, or his body the whole time." I am not sufficient of a dramatic critic to measure the value of this hint, but I should, in fairness, add that at this point our critics felt that the composer had set his actors an almost impossible task, the dialogue between the characters, and especially father and child, being sometimes most unnaturally lengthened by the slow music to which it is set.

On Edith Clegg, as the mother, I also noted but one remark ; it was sympathetically directed to her difficulties with a stage door that would fly open, and that embarrassed her as it had previously embarrassed her daughter. " Very disturbing to everybody on the stage and in the audience. Somebody'll get it hot for that after the show's over," I overheard, but

I was able to assure my friends that in opera those little trifles lead to no recriminations. On my taking heart to grumble likewise at the instability of the houses in Paris, which ripple from doorstep to chimney-pot when the front door is thoughtlessly banged by any hasty visitor, I received little sympathy. I was told of David Belasco's solid oak-panelled interior in some play then running in New York, and also of massive doors and door-frames packed in huge crates with which the company to which my friends belong had recently travelled, but it was made clear to me that the luxury of rigid architecture is neither mechanically nor commercially possible in the case of an opera company playing not one piece, but a dozen, and these changed from day to day. I was sorry to hear it, for I have never felt happy about this operatic jerry-building.

The close of Act II, Scene I, where (the stage being cleared, but for the hero in silent meditation at the front) an Old Clothes Man passes at the back, with his musical trade-cry, struck our critics as very poetic, and they reverted to it in conversation many times during the evening. "That Clothes Man's part is perfect," they said. "It's all *fat*! And *what* an ending for a scene!" But they surmised (and with truth) that a touch of the poetry had been lost by the fall of the curtain a few seconds before its time—an accident that should have been avoided.

I neglected to ask for an opinion on the "Oh, Paris!" prayer, in which the hero and heroine of the piece (who, though in love, have hitherto behaved pretty much like normal people in a world of hard fact) fall

in inspired rapture on their knees and worship the
glimmering lights of the outspread city.   But I remember that from a glance at their faces I thought that
my companions felt the cheap sentimentality of this.
The whole of the festal part of the Montmartre scene,
with its crowds of people moving about the stage, they
pronounced to be extremely well carried out, but at
the end, where, at nightfall, the daughter is called
home by the mother to save the life of the sick father,
I heard the lady mutter that, despite the urgency of the
summons, it was only in opera that a girl would go
across Paris as she was, and without even troubling
to put on her hat or throw on a shawl.

Adverse comment throughout the evening was given
to the lighting.   The working-class homes, and even
the gay Bohemian haunts, were, my friends argued,
very imperfectly illuminated, and a certain slight lack
of point and spirit throughout the evening they put
down to the subtle influence on both actors and audience
of continual half-lights, even in the scenes which would
properly admit of some brilliance.   Their plea, then,
was for a Brighter Paris.   In this matter the complaint
became continual and pressing.   I have however heard
that the explanation is that the Covent Garden scenery
for this piece is so worn out that the stage-manager
dare not let us see it clearly.

It will be seen that the general tenor of professional
comment on our opera company was by no means
unfavourable, and, indeed, having enjoyed my interested hospitality the other evening, my companions,
who had not previously visited Covent Garden during
the season, or seen before our new National Com-

pany, were overheard to congratulate one another on the fact that they had already, on their own initiative, and as members of the general paying public, secured places for the performance of " Siegfried " the following evening. I hope that of this also they will be able to give me a good report. I shall especially inquire as to the behaviour of the dragon, whose deathbed repentance, with Wagner as his spiritual director, is rarely as convincing as a good moralist would wish it to be.

IV. DEBUSSY AND " DASH "

I once recorded in my account of the week's music in London the dictum of a lady whose conversation I involuntarily overheard at the Covent Garden performance of " Pelléas et Mélisande." She preferred, she said, " an opera with more dash in it." She is, I am sure, by no means alone in her very allowable preference; indeed, from observations that night of people around me, I should say she was ordained by Providence as the mouthpiece of a large number of otherwise inarticulate sufferers, crystallizing into a few well-chosen words what they, with their inferior gifts of expression, were compelled to leave floating about their minds as mere vague, misty feeling. She said, indeed, precisely the same thing as Romain Rolland, when, after praising " Pelléas " as one of " the most perfect flowerings of the French spirit," and advising foreigners who wish to understand that spirit to study Racine on the one hand, and Debussy on the other, he adds : " Non pas que l'art de Debussy, pas plus que celui de Racine, suffise à représenter le génie française. Il y a un tout autre coté de ce génie, qui n'est nullement représenté ici : c'est l'action héroïque, l'ivresse de la raison, le rire, la passion de la lumière, la France de Rabelais, de Molière, de Diderot, et en musique, dirons nous (faute de mieux) la France de Berlioz et de Bizet." And then (and this is the point) he adds : " *Pour dire la vérité c'est celle que je préfère.*"

What is it, then, that our friend needs to know in order to enjoy " Pelléas," which, not having been heard in this country for some years, comes to her, as to many others, as a novelty ? Well, my dear good woman, get right out of your mind all the other operas you have ever heard and listen to this with a brain freed of all prepossessions as to what an opera should be like. " Pelléas " is unique. There is not a single work in the repertory with which you can compare it. Secondly, study—no, that is too hard a word— read and enjoy Maeterlinck's play itself. If you do not like reading French, you can, through any bookseller, get for a couple of shillings Laurence Alma Tadema's translation. I can hardly believe that anyone yet has really understood and taken pleasure in a work so entirely original in conception and style as " Pelléas " without a preliminary reading of the play ; they ought to sell it in the theatre, as they do the trumpery thirty-page pamphlet libretto of " Les Pécheurs de Perles," which costs the same money, and as a piece of literature is worthless. Of course, nobody can read a play in the theatre, but a few perhaps would read it when they got home in order to understand what the opera had been about and then they might come again !

Having read the play (it is, by the way, quite short), you will realize that it is one that will not make an opera of physical action, but rather an opera of mental states. There is, indeed, but one true murder in the whole thing (but one, that is, which a coroner's jury could condemn), and that, as a matter of fact, is found in performance to be the one really ineffective thing in the opera, so that you wish that, like the ancient Greeks, Maeterlinck and Debussy would do their murders behind the scenes, and only show us their results. If you insist on physical violence, Verdi and Puccini and others will supply you with it in abundance. Even if you insist on the violent expression of emotions, you had better go to them. "Pelléas" is an opera of reticence—of passion, but passion the realization of which is to take place rather in your imagination than on the stage. (This, you see, is an opera which flatters you by attributing to you the possession of imagination ; not all operas, by any means, pay you this compliment.)

There are lots of other things I might say about "Pelléas," but I have not the space to say them, and really, having observed from your face the other night that, despite your rather startling remark, you are really a person of good intelligence, I realize that it is hardly necessary to do so. One important thing, however, I must explain—the music. This is neither an alternation of recitatives and formal arias (as in, say, Mozart), nor a symphonic working up of " leading motives " (as in Wagner), nor a musical painting of the surface of the play (as in Puccini, who, you will recall, in " Bohème " provides three or four *pizzicato* string notes, one for each drop of water that Rodolfo is to throw on the face of the fainting Mimi). The voice part of " Pelléas " is the nearest thing to the inflections of speech that has ever been attempted : it derives from plain-chant, not from Italian recitative. Here, as an example, are the opening words :

GOLAUD.
Je ne pourrai plus sor-tir de cet-te fo . rêt !

The music never rises into continuous lyrical passages, such as could be chopped out and sold separately in the music-shops as songs.   Even a passage like the following (see next page), which has something of a lyrical quality, is a rare thing (this passage, by the way, is somewhat compressed here, and the parts to some extent inverted to get it into " short score ") :

The composer has, indeed, simply tried to absorb Maeterlinck's work into himself and to give it out again with its emotions intensified by music.   There is plenty of lovely melody and harmony, but its loveliness is bound up with that of the poet's thought— it has no separate existence ; it is a Siamese twin.

So now you know, partially, what to expect and (even more important) what not to expect. Your mistake has been in going to hear " Pelléas " and expecting another " Carmen."   I don't myself much like

" Carmen " (that is, I don't admire it as some of my
colleagues do, who reckon it one of the world's greatest
masterpieces of dramatic-musical art). Very likely
my mistake is the converse of yours.   You go to hear

a " Pelléas " and expect a " Carmen " ; I go to hear
a " Carmen " and expect a " Pelléas." We are both of
us wrong and will make up our minds to do better in
future.   The judicious Rolland shall be our model.

A HAUNTED HEAD

AMONGST really well-brought-up people it is usually considered bad form to swear at a parson. Why, I do not quite know. I can see great objection in the case of a mild-mannered and gentle Nonconformist, but in that of an Anglican, who on every twenty-second evening of the month is accustomed to hear his choir and people express themselves in the vigorous language of a more robust age, why should these precautions be taken? Yet custom constrains me, and I am held back by courtesy from saying all I think about the genial Precentor of Hereford.

What have I against the Precentor? Just this—Some time ago I published an article or two in which I discussed some manifestations of musical instinct in the very young. Seeing these, the Precentor (whose intentions were admirable) sent me for my study the two little music manuscript books in which the great Ouseley's mother recorded, day by day, and week by week, his juvenile outpourings. These books are remarkable, and as, according to inquiries I made, they were supposed to have been long lost, their re-discovery was of interest. St. Michael's College, Tenbury (Ouseley's foundation), used to have a copy of them, but I understand it has disappeared. That of the Precentor of Hereford has, I believe, since it left my hands, been deposited in the library of Christ Church, Oxford (Ouseley's *alma mater*), where it will receive the same care and protection as the many musical treasures already placed there by old Dean Aldrich a couple of centuries ago and by others since. The Precentor's loan set me on a little course of Ouseley reading. I searched Messrs. Blackwell's resourceful establishment in the Broad at Oxford, and found a copy of Havergal's "Memorials of Frederick Arthur Gore Ouseley, Baronet, M.A., Doctor and Professor of Music in the University of Oxford," and, later, Joyce's "Life," and was soon deep in contemplation of the wonders of the childhood of a musician of whom it is recorded that "when suffering the greatest pains from teething, an air on the pianoforte was sure to stop his crying," and who (a year or two later) would casually remark to you that it thundered in G, or the wind whistled in D, or the clock chimed in B minor. The following anecdote is representative of a good many given in the records. It refers to the boy's fifth year:

"As he was sitting between two young ladies, his papa happened to have a bad cold, when he said to them, 'Only think, papa blows his nose in G,' which occasioned a roar of laughter."

The actual compositions of little Ouseley interested me a good deal. Of course, they reflect the style of the period, and what he heard his sisters playing on the drawing-room piano was imitated in what he himself composed and got them or his mother to write down for him. But the following is not bad for a child not quite six years of age, is it ?

The great J. B. Logier (" Professor of Music and Originator of a System of Musical Instruction which met with merited success in England and Ireland, although more qualified in the latter—but most particularly in Prussia, where it triumphed over opposition and obtained royal and ministerial protection and patronage ") wrote to the composer's father highly commending the young musician's efforts, one of which he thought " really a very elegant and pathetic little composition," while another, he says, brought tears to his eyes. The Professor seems to have been rather susceptible, but in the main he is right, and the wonder is that a musicianship that began so brilliantly should have ended so tamely, groping at last in a thickish fog of academicism, and producing, amongst much that was dignified and genuinely artistic, a good deal that was merely scientific and correct.

But I am straying from my original intention, which was to tell you why I nurse a grudge against an honoured dignitary of the Church and practitioner of our musical art. Turning over the leaves of Havergal and Joyce, browsing on their delightful anecdotes of the double-bass player who excused himself from rehearsal because he had " mislaid his instrument " ; the choir member who, charged with spoiling the service, replied : " No, it was the organ, Sir Frederick, that played out of tune " ; the lady who, having heard Ouseley play the overture to " Esther," thanked him for " that beautiful *chorus* of Handel's," and, being corrected, replied : " Indeed, I think I ought to know, considering my great-aunt once heard Handel play on the organ " ; the after-dinner entertainment provided for the Oxford Professor of Music by his host, consisting of the " Hallelujah Chorus," arranged for three flutes ; the musical vicarage which welcomed him by setting six musical boxes going at the same time, and so forth, I at last arrived at the account of the compositions sent to Sir Frederick by well-meaning amateurs desirous of winning his high approval. And then there caught my eye a striking double-chant written by " a musical lady " and posted to our Baronet-Precentor-Professor with the intimation that its composer had " got it done in our Parish Church last Sunday."

Heads can be haunted as well as houses, and my sufferings over that little piece of inspired sacred expression have been greater than any of Mark Twain with his " pink trip slip for a two cent fare, punch in the presence of the passengare." Punch, indeed !

I would like to do a little punching. But one cannot punch a Precentor, and all I can do is to warn my readers *on no account* to break their household peace by trying that chant on their piano. The grip of those strains upon the musical memory is violent and unrelaxing. Once hear the tune and it sings through your mind at bed and at board, it hinders your business, it makes you walk the street to its lilting rhythm.

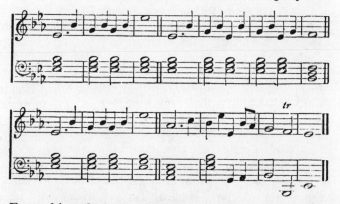

Everything that you ever heard of Bach, Beethoven, Wagner, and the gentle Stravinsky is banished from your memory, and you find yourself spending your life as it were in a parish church of the eighteen-fifties, condemned for ever to feel your very heart beating and your lungs moving to the inspired melody, and surely no less inspired harmony, of that " Musical Lady."

THE MUSIC OR THE MAKING?

I. SILK PURSES AND SOWS' EARS

CAN a fine piece of music be made out of poor themes? The editor of the "Musical Times" thinks it can. The question came into his pages in this way. Our violinist, Miss Kathleen Parlow, on a tour in the United States, had been interviewed by "Musical America," and had taken the opportunity of expressing her opinion of London musical criticism. As an instance of its errors, she complained that when she gave the first London performance of the Pizzetti sonata, "it raised pandemonium amongst the critics." To this the editor of the "Musical Times," in a justifiably stern reproof, replies:

Now, as a matter of fact, of all the new works produced in London that year, few, if any, had a more favourable reception from the critics than this sonata, so much so that Mr. Scholes has during the past few days been moved to make an attempt to show that the laudatory critics and public were wrong. He does this by quoting the motives, and calling attention to their poverty. But there are too many examples of fine works evolved from insignificant material to make this method other than risky. It is judging at the wrong end. The proof of the pud-

110

ding lies in the eating thereof, not in a critical dissection and inspection of its ingredients.

Now, as a matter of fact, I was most careful throughout my Pizzetti article to make it clear that I was not condemning the sonata merely on its themes, and gave much more space to description of the treatment of the themes than I did to discussion of the themes themselves. I was careful about this because I knew that perhaps nine musicians out of ten at present hold the view I myself once unthinkingly held—that in music not the text but the sermon is what matters, and that numbers of masterpieces exist " evolved " (as it is put above) from " insignificant material." I hinted that it would be interesting at some future time " to discuss together the general statement that you cannot make silk purses out of sows' ears " ; the editor of the " Musical Times " abandoned my metaphor and substituted another, which will serve equally well. In effect, he states this, and nothing less : " Good puddings can be made out of poor ingredients." I deny it, and with me I think would stand the gracious lady who ministers to his creature comforts.

I think my former mistake, and Mr. Harvey Grace's present one, turn upon a confused use of that very word " insignificant." We are accustomed to acclaim the genius of Bach and Beethoven in the production of resounding fugues and stirring symphonies out of simple thematic material. But " simplicity " is, of course, no synonym for "insignificance," and having well pondered and examined afresh a large portion of the output of the two composers mentioned (whom I pick for the purpose partly because I mentioned them in the article referred to, and partly because admittedly they, if anyone, could achieve the suggested alchemistic transmutation of baser into higher elements), I am prepared to make this assertion—There do *not* exist cases where a first-rate piece of music has been fashioned out of poor or " insignificant " material.

Two very arguable instances are the opening themes of Beethoven's third and fifth symphonies. But let me give the opening theme of the third, at first as it stands (simple but strong), and then with the most trifling changes (yet now weak and " insignificant ") :

Beethoven made a great movement out of (*a*). Could he have done so out of (*b*) ? With all reverence I say he probably could not. Observe similarly the opening theme of the fifth symphony, and here also consider an alternative :

Again I suggest that even Beethoven could have made nothing great out of that so slightly changed but so vastly weakened alternative.[1] But, indeed, the care

---

[1] It does occur, admittedly, in the development portion of the movement, but not, I think, in such a way as to weaken the force of my argument.

Beethoven took in the composition (for we may use that word) of his little germ-themes ought to be sufficient to show us that it does matter much to a composer what material he uses. As is well known, a simple Beethoven theme is sometimes found to occur again and again in his sketch-books, over a long term of years, beginning often in a comparatively weak and "insignificant" form, but growing up to strength and abounding "significance." In the sonatas Beethoven's opening themes, especially, are enormously "significant" (by which I take it we intend to say, "charged with actual and potential meaning"). He is like Bacon, who in his essays almost always breaks ground with a striking and suggestive phrase—as, for example (" Of Truth "), " What is truth ? said jesting Pilate, and would not stay for an answer " ; or (" Of Marriage and Single Life "), " He that hath wife and children hath given hostages to fortune " ; or (" Of Riches "), " I cannot call riches better than the Baggage of Virtue." Open the volume of the Beethoven sonatas and note the similarly striking openings of Nos, 1, 2, 5, 9, 10, and 11 (to go no farther). I do not say that all these movements are equally fine ; an indifferent coat *may* be made out of the best broadcloth, though a good coat cannot be made out of shoddy.

As for the Bach (or other) fugues, our editor has Browning with him :

> First you deliver your phrase,
>   Nothing propound that I see
> Fit in itself for much blame or much praise.

But here is this same confusion between simplicity and

insignificance.   Look at fugue 4 (C sharp minor) of the
" 48."   Its subject is a mere four notes ; but these have
shape (a " sequence "), and how " significant " that rise
of a diminished fourth between the two little two-note
motives that make up the four-note phrase ! Now look
at fugue 25 (C major) ; here we have a long but " insignificant " subject—and a dull fugue.   At some of the
elements that contribute to " strength " or " weakness "
in a theme I have hinted in a later chapter, " What
is Melody ? "   One of these is climax ; the subject of
fugue 4 has it.   The subject of fugue 25 has it not—
or rather, having, in its second bar, brought forth a
climax, it proceeds at once to kill it.

II.   SOMETHING FROM NOTHING ?

How much of the new music heard by us in London
concert-rooms will be heard there by our grandchildren ?
How much of that heard by our grandparents is now
heard by us ?   Taking it all into account (orchestral
music, choral music, chamber music, piano music, songs),
I should say not one-half of one per cent.   Why ?   For
various reasons.   Much of it had no real initial artistic
impulse behind it—was just " made."   But, the lack
of impulse being the first cause of failure, what was
wrong with this music as music ?   One or both of two
things : there is weakness either in the making or in
the material, and more often in the material, for the technique of " making " can be fairly well taught in any
school of music, whereas the material is the gift of
heaven—in its germinal form, at any rate.   It will be

seen, then, that the above-mentioned discussion between
the editor of the " Musical Times " and myself was not
merely of academic interest, but had an intensely practical bearing. In the issue of that paper which followed
the appearance of my " Silk Purse " article, which the
reader has just considered, it was boldly stated that
" the composer more than any other creative artist
has the power of evolving something from nothing."
Here, I think, is an admirably candid admission of the
acceptance of a very dangerous doctrine.

My friend gave as one of his examples illustrating his
" Something from Nothing " theory, Bach's popular
Organ Toccata in F. I mentioned by number certain
of Bach's piano fugues, showing how strong (though
often simple) their subjects were, and also making it
clear that, in my judgment, in the few cases where the
subjects were less strong the fugues were less good. I
was pleased to see that this point was largely conceded.
What both that editor and I believe about fugues has, I
have just recalled, been expressed before us. Sir Henry
Hadow's words (in his British Academy Beethoven
lecture) would be endorsed by us both :

" What is the difference between a fugue of Bach
and a fugue of Marpurg ? Not the command of
counterpoint, for Marpurg's is perfect : an ' adequate '
than which, in Croce's phrase, ' there cannot be a
more adequate.' It is that Marpurg's theme is an
academic text, the meaning of which is exhausted
in its adaptability to contrapuntal display, whereas
Bach's theme is a quickening spirit, which is not
only alive itself, but a radiating centre of life
through the whole composition. It is the difference

between a good copy of Latin verse and a page of Virgil."

But there, I think, is laid down a principle that can be applied as much to sonata form as to fugue form, and as the passage quoted occurs in a discussion of Beethoven, I need hardly point out that its author is of my mind. There is perhaps a superficial plausibility, but I think nothing more, in the " Musical Times " view that " a sonata movement is so largely a matter of development that a long work may be concerned more with the derivatives of the subjects than with the subjects themselves, whereas the essence of the fugal form lies in its insistence on the subject, presented (usually without change) in a constantly varying polyphonic texture." A stream does not rise higher than its fount, and the derivatives of a theme are not likely to be better than the theme itself. But to discuss this needs a chapter or two to itself, and in order that I may some time do so, perhaps my courteous antagonist will some day give me five or six examples of what he considers fine sonata form movements evolved from what he considers poor thematic material. But even in the case of the fugue itself it was evident that he would consider that the Hadow view just quoted must not be too strictly insisted upon, for he said, " Bach has once or twice done wonders with trifling material." I wish that such words as " trifling " and " insignificant " might have been dropped out of this discussion, and that we might have kept rigidly to the antitheses " strong " and " weak," or " fine " and " poor," or " good " and " bad." I believe the confusion of *simplicity* with *poverty* is a frequent cause of confusion.

As an example of a fine piece evolved from " insignificant motives," the " Musical Times " mentioned Bach's popular Organ Toccata in F—" a gigantic movement of four hundred and thirty-eight bars, derived from these two insignificant motives " :

My quondam antagonist is an organist, and I differ from him (and probably from many of his colleagues) since I think this Toccata, however " gigantic," one of Bach's poorer pieces. I know how any player enjoys the rolling of his diapasons, and the rapid scurrying up and down the manuals, and I am sure that the gymnastic exercises of those long solo pedal sequences must be physically very good for one, but I would point out that a good deal of this piece is mere noisy excitement. And note that the weak places in the piece are exactly those where the germ-theme, in itself melodically and rhythmically strong, is strangely weakened by the composer into real " insignificance."   Surely, to any keenly critical ear, there must come disappointment when, after this bold and vigorous opening :

there succeeds a treatment of the initial motive in so watered a form as this :

As soon as that sort of thing begins (and there is a good deal of it here and there in the piece) the " punch " has gone out of the playing. Had Bach begun with that weaker form of his theme, and made his piece from that, instead of mainly from the stronger form, I do not think we should find Mr. Harvey Grace and his organ-playing friends so fond of Bach's famous Toccata in F, nor their congregations so willing to stay after service to hear it. I am, then, nothing shaken in my conviction that though a great composer can do more with poor material than one who is less great, even the very greatest of all can make no " silk purses out of sows' ears " (to use again one of my metaphors), no " good puddings from poor ingredients " (to use again one of my friend's). It comes, I think, to this : Bach or Beethoven, two of the greatest chancellors of the musical exchequer the world has known, have perhaps sometimes given us what looks like " Sixpence for Fourpence," but not even they have ever contrived to produce for us " Something from Nothing." The practical application is obvious, and I hope our younger composers, our budding Bachs and blossoming Beethovens, will duly note it.

WHAT IS MELODY?

WHAT makes a tune ? An article by Mr. Edwin Evans, in the " Musical News and Herald," " About Melody," some time ago, raised the question, and I realized at once that it was one which had vaguely bothered me since small boyhood, for I can remember, when very young, sitting in church, Sunday by Sunday, and spending the non-singing portion of the service in thinking over the hymn-tune just heard and wondering what gave it its force. It seemed to me, as I recall, that there was a sort of conversation going on—one little interval or phrase answered by another, a going-up followed by another going-up or countered by a going-down, every motion seeming to have behind it a sense of purpose that was easier to realize than to define. I did not know anything of " Crowd Psychology " in those days, or I might have used Le Bon's term to express to myself the nature of the mystery ; here were ordinary single notes brought into a group and at once working together with a common purpose, and taking on some curious fresh character of a communal kind. And yet this did not always and necessarily happen when notes were brought together, for keys struck successively at random on the piano often refused to co-operate ; they did not assume the crowd mind, but remained mere private individuals. This childish problem is obviously fundamental.

The essence of the " Musical News " theory lies in the following passage :

I have long felt that the only tenable definition of melody is a succession of single notes so arranged that their mutual relations are those to which the ear is accustomed—in short, that melody is our recognition of the familiar. The ear grows inured to certain inflections, sequences of notes, and *bouts de phrases*, and when these are present in sufficient number to create a suggestion of old friendship, but at the same time their arrangement conveys a feeling of freshness, the result to the average man is melody. . . . I would even go so far as to say that there is no such thing as melody in the abstract. It is the creation not of sound, but of habit.

In other words, we can class the material of our new music as " cooking," " fresh," or " new laid," but the classification will vary with different consumers, whose previous egg-experiences are of different kinds. But if the degree of " freshness " is the deciding factor, how is it that a good tune does not deteriorate as it becomes familiar ? The " Old Hundredth," when I first heard it as a child, would be classifiable as " new laid," but, according to this theory, would now have become (for me) not merely " cooking," but actually stale. And it has not done so. Conversely, the most heterogeneous collection of notes frequently repeated ought to become to me a melody, and I cannot believe this would happen. Then the theory seems to leave no room at all for variations of intrinsic " quality," and we all know that " quality " (as a quite distinct thing from degree of familiarity) does exist.

I take it that the proper way to arrive at a safe theory as to the nature of melody would be to take a very large number of examples, of all races and periods, and to find their common factors. In this article I can take but one or two. Here is a universally popular Welsh folk-tune :

Every one who hears it feels it to be, not merely a beautiful, but a perfect tune. Driven to examine it, in order to explain to myself its appeal, I come to the conclusion that this lies largely in (*a*) economy and (*b*) climax. Look at it really closely, take it to bits, and, as regards (*a*), you will find that the whole thing is made out of a little step-wise motif of three notes, used at various pitches, generally descending, but sometimes, for the sake of variety, made to ascend. This motif will be found at least ten times in those twelve bars. Now, look at this (also, I feel, a beautiful melody) from the opening of " The Rite of Spring " :

Again, we have this "economy," the opening motif being repeated many times, with skilfully varied rhythm. I should guess, then, that "economy" is, if not an essential element, at least one of the several elements, of which some at least must be present, to give the sense of unity which partly distinguishes melody from no-melody, but that, with all the unity, there must be also some measure of variety.

Now look carefully again at both those melodies. I think it will be found that in both cases their "melodiousness" gains enormously from the fact that each, after moving for some time on the lower ranges, rises (once, and once only, as it happens, in these examples) to a higher note. In other words, both tunes have *climax* (cf. page 84, where a melody of Beethoven is given, with a similar climax, but on a *low* note). Now examine another example, the opening phrase of Stravinsky's second piece of the " Three Pieces for Clarinet Alone " :

Here, again, if you will analyse the tune carefully, you will find a similar "economy," But as to the climax, which seems to be intended here to come at the very end, I think you will feel that the composer has enormously weakened his effect by immediately anticipating his climactic note. This is still a " tune," but a rather poorer tune, or, as I think it could be better expressed, *less a tune*. A factor common to all three examples, which helps to make them " melodies " and not mere collections of notes, is relation to a centre or " tonic," or note of tonal rest ; the central note of the first example is G, of the second C, of the third D (in three octaves). Briefly, then, three out of a possibly large number of qualifications for acceptance as melody are (*a*) economy, (*b*) climax, and (*c*) intelligible and felt relation to a tonic. I should guess that the very interesting theory of my friend whom I have quoted has really little application to the distinction between " tune " and " no-tune." But it may have a bearing (and possibly a large one) upon another question—the problem of " scale," "key," "mode." In other words, it does not explain to us the building, but it may explain the geological formations from which the stones are hewn.

SOME NOTES ON SCRIABIN

RUMMAGING lately amongst various pre-war and early-war documents in my files, I came across a quantity of material on Scriabin, the possession of which I had forgotten. Some of this seems to me to be of considerable interest. The longest treatment we then had of the subject (of any value) was the excellent but necessarily rather brief chapter in Mr. Montagu-Nathan's " Contemporary Russian Composers." Mr. Swan's book on Scriabin has since appeared, but is quite brief. In these circumstances the publication of a collection of odd notes upon the composer may be welcome. I have tried to classify these in some logical order, so as to make them readable, and of service for something more than the mere desultory satisfaction of curiosity. As many of the particulars given have certainly never before been published in this country, I think that they may be of some value to students and to the many keen spirits who now flock together whenever a Scriabin piano recital or the performance of a Scriabin orchestral work is announced. For the translation of which I have made use I am indebted to my friend, Mr. S. W. Pring, whose name may be recalled by some of my readers as that of the translator of Griboyedof's classic comedy, " Gore ot Ouma " (" The Misfortune of being Clever ").

In giving English readers this work, Mr. Pring rendered a service to British lovers of Russian literature that should be remembered. It is a curious fact that whereas one could, in 1914, have found a translation of some kind of every other Russian literary classic that had attained real popularity in the vernacular, Griboyedof's work should, for some ninety years, have been neglected. When the first English stage performance of this comedy was given during the Birmingham Russia Week, it was, of course, Mr. Pring's version that was used. For some time I was fortunate in having with Mr. Pring a friendly arrangement by which I procured for him from Russia all the musical literature he demanded, whilst in return he gave me a translation or précis of everything in it of real interest. Then the war reached the point where communication with Russia became too difficult, and the arrangement dropped.

In addition to acknowledging the help of Mr. Pring, I have to thank Mr. Montagu-Nathan, who (Mr. Pring being then in Central Africa) went critically through the material, and, moreover, verified it by occasional references to the Russian original in places where the typist, who, some years ago, deciphered Mr. Pring's quite microscopic script for me, had very obviously gone astray.

I. Scriabin as Student

Scriabin's definite academic training was, of course, received at the Moscow Conservatory. Here his teachers were Taneyef for counterpoint, Arensky for composition, and Safonof for piano. The teaching and personality of Taneyef were probably quite acceptable to him, and so, certainly, were those of Safonof. From Arensky he seems quickly to have taken an aversion, and his work for him was done under compulsion. On one occasion Arensky set him as a summer holiday task the writing of ten fugues. Of these he wrote but two—a fugue-nocturne and a five-part fugue. This last was a few years ago in the possession of E. K. Rozenof; it is described as undistinguished in theme and in treatment, but as containing, in its stretto, original touches suggestive of the later Scriabin. When, leaving the stricter style of fugue, Scriabin went on to free composition, he gave still more annoyance to his master. If Arensky asked for one thing, Scriabin would invariably bring another. As one instance, Arensky told his pupil to write an orchestral scherzo—result, the composition of an introduction to an opera on a Lithuanian subject. Speaking to another of his students, Arensky described Scriabin as " a madman." In later notes will be found some support for the use of this word in something approaching its literal sense. Allowing fully for the facts that (*a*) to the sober British mind the average Russian must almost necessarily appear to be a very incompletely self-controlled person, and that (*b*) genius of any nationality often shows itself a stranger to the *convenances* of normal everyday life, there nevertheless seems evident in Scriabin's whole career a rather specially marked lack of balance, showing itself, for example, in an almost Beethovenish capacity for quarrelling with his best friends. In the case of

Scriabin's relations with Arensky there were, however, in all probability faults on both sides and a general lack of " give and take," and finally Scriabin left his Conservatory course incomplete and departed without a diploma. In the document before me one of the characteristic traits of Scriabin's mind right through life is gently but neatly epitomized : " Scriabin's belief in himself was so profound that when he encountered those whose attitude towards him was one of distrust or repudiation, he invariably considered them to be in the wrong, and henceforth ceased to appreciate them." In this small particular, however, we are all, perhaps, in greater or lesser measure, Scriabins.

Taneyef, it is satisfactory to find, understood Scriabin and gave him a far better name. He spoke of him as a quick learner who always did the exercises that were set, but admits that he was not particularly fond of work, and was ingenious in finding short cuts, " such as selecting the shortest themes for treatment as exercises in ' imitation ' " ! Some R.A.M. and R.C.M. professors to-day could doubtless give a similarly qualified approval of youthful genius under their charge.

Safonof's recollections of Scriabin seem to have been invariably pleasant. He described as one of the finest experiences of his life an occasion when, whilst giving Scriabin a piano lesson, being over-tired, he dropped off to sleep and woke to hear a D flat major prelude until then unknown to him. He remained spellbound and afraid to move or speak lest he should break the spell. I take this to be a reference to Op. 11, No. 15 (one of the twenty-four Preludes), that simple, slowly moving piece, of but a page in length, written entirely in the middle register of the piano, and very mystic in feeling.

On another occasion, as Safonof related, he awoke to hear an improvisation—" again one of my most exquisite musical delights—since Rubinstein ! "

II. SCRIABIN'S PROCESSES OF COMPOSITION

I am often interested and amused to discover the ideas of the general public as to the way in which a piece of music comes into existence. Generally it will be found that others than the musically trained have a vague notion that something called " inspiration " accounts for all. The careful selection of musical themes, the thoughtful planning of general design (the relation of one part to another and of each part to the whole), the laborious redrafting of passages that on reflection are felt to be ineffective, the putting the work aside in order that one may come to it again with a " fresh eye," or the slogging at it for days and weeks and the trying to eliminate what one feels to be faults, the shortening this part and lengthening that and rescoring the other—the mere possibility of all this has never entered the head of the average listener, who will be found, on inquiry, to have a vague picture in his mind of a frenzied composer at the piano thumping out a masterpiece as heaven sends it to him and then turning to his table to write out what he has played, or some other picture equally untrue to the usual facts of the composer's life. Some day I should like to write a book or a series of articles on " How Composers Work," with illustrations from the practice of Beethoven, with his sketch-books always in his pockets or by his bedside for the recording of the tiny scraps of inspiration that came to him ; of Brahms, sweating and toiling at a piece " until there is not a note too much or too little " ; of Elgar, working out his schemes in his head as he strides over Hampstead Heath, and only putting pen to paper when the last detail has been decided upon, after, perhaps, weeks of hard thought ; of Vaughan Williams, with two or three successive versions of the " London Symphony," modestly going about and begging friends who had heard the first version to tell him what to cut out, and issuing the last one ruthlessly pruned and compressed, and with one of the two original trios of its scherzo altogether removed. Here I must not develop this general idea, but I think it may be of interest to describe, in a page or two, Scriabin's practice.

Like Beethoven, Scriabin had his stock of notebooks in which he jotted down his ideas and rough sketches for his compositions. " He was very fond of showing and playing what he had composed, even if it were not quite finished, and he often made corrections and alterations—not always for the better. For instance, the Polonaise in B flat minor, in its present form, is quite unlike the original composition. Usually he made very few sketches for his piano pieces ; he played them to others in various stages of completion, and did not commit them to writing until they were almost finished." The Polonaise mentioned is, I suppose, the Op. 21, which was published by Belaieff in 1898, when the composer was twenty-seven. It is a brilliant but fairly commonplace piece of " salon music," and strikes me as an early piece which has strayed out of its true opus number order. Scriabin " would talk of a composition as though it actually existed, when only a movement, or even an episode, was actually composed ; he would play the germ of a composition, a few bars, a single harmony, Apparently it helped him to formulate the composition in his mind, so that when he took pen and paper he was able, for the most part, to write it straight away (especially in the case of the pianoforte works). Nevertheless, a definite number of bars, or even pages, were often left blank, as he did not always know *how* they would be filled, though he always knew that they *would* be filled, and how many there would be. In spite of all this, he sometimes worried for days over some small detail."

Like many other composers, Scriabin was convinced that his latest composition was his best, and considering the fairly rapid and regular progress he shows from quite simple methods (harmonic and other) to much more complex methods, this is not a surprise. From this resulted his taking no interest whatever in the later " arrangement " or " transcription " of his orchestral pieces, although, in their time, they might have been his favourites. " For instance, L. E. Konius transcribed the ' Ecstasy ' for two pianos (four hands) and the Third Symphony (also four hands), but Scriabin did not even care to look through these arrangements before they were printed. Scriabin's publishers always announced on his orchestral scores, ' Piano arrangement by the Composer ; price —,' considering themselves entitled to expect that Scriabin would undertake the task, but he never did so, except in the case of the Piano Concerto."

Of course, the preference for a few specially significant compositions lasted even when they were no longer new. Amongst these was the Seventh Sonata, apparently first played, so far as London is concerned, in 1921, by Mr. Edward Mitchell, and then strangely found by some of the critics to be puzzling in form. Scriabin called this his " White Mass," and considered it the nearest approximation to the great " Mystery " which was to have been the culmination of his life and work. He ranked the Eighth Sonata high, on account of its harmonic attainments ; the Sixth and the Tenth, my document states, he himself never succeeded in learning—a statement which surprises me, and one wherein I suspect the existence of some mistake, a suspicion strongly confirmed by one or two of Scriabin's familiar associates and others in touch with Russian music, whom I have questioned, including Mr. Swan. " Vers la Flamme," Op. 72, was, by the way, to have been also a sonata. Another work the composer greatly loved was the First Symphony, in which we meet with the attempt to use the purely mental, or ideal, as the foundation of the musical edifice, and see that effort to connect sound with thought, music with philosophy and religion, which becomes more and more characteristic of Scriabin's work. Konius relates that Scriabin would not part with the score of this work, even at night, but took it to bed with him. (I recall that it is recorded somewhere that in earlier life Chopin's works were placed under his pillow in the same way.) For this First Symphony he made pianoforte sketches, a custom which he subsequently abandoned. Scriabin's philosophical ideas I touch on later. It will be found, I think, that these need not be taken with enormous seriousness, but it is obviously impossible to put altogether on one side influences which permeated a composer's whole musical life and work.

III. SCRIABIN AND "LAW"

The special feature of a recent London piano recital, already alluded to, was what was announced as the first London performance of the Seventh Sonata. If the announcement was correct (and I have no recollection that contradicts it), there was some reason for astonishment. For the Seventh Sonata was Scriabin's own favourite amongst his works, and, so far as my own present opinion goes, this is reasonably justifiable favouritism. In an article in a musical paper a year or two ago, Mr. Montagu-Nathan, pleading for a fair consideration of Scriabin's output, admitted in closing : " No music is immortal : Scriabin's will probably not have a very long life." It may be so. Nobody can say. But for myself, I shared the feelings of a correspondent, who said that even when unable fully to grasp a new work, one could often feel it to be *true*, and for the moment, with the recollection of Mr. Mitchell's very spirited playing still lingering in my mind, I find it difficult not to think of the Seventh Sonata as a lasting master-work. Perhaps for the moment I am rather " carried away."

What is it that, for some people, constitutes the difficulty in accepting this work ? After acquaintance with the Fifth and Sixth Sonatas, the Seventh comes as no great stranger. I note that a colleague on one of the dailies said, speaking of this recital: " The Seventh Sonata of Scriabin appears the negation of all law." I cannot understand the phrase. From the point of view of formal construction, the sonata is very regular. It is true it has not quite the cut-and-dried plan of a late Haydn or Mozart or an earlier Beethoven work, but its principles of construction are exactly the same as those of all the classical composers. There are quite definite " subjects," and the whole work is made out of these, by the sound and established processes of contrast, development, and restatement. In matters of form Scriabin was no wild innovator ; he came to fulfil rather than to destroy the existing " law." His method of laying out a work is but a slight and very reasonable extension of that of Beethoven or Brahms. So far as this matter of " form " is concerned, he is in the old succession, and no founder of a new dynasty. What, then, is it that retards appreciation and brings it about that one of the most experienced critics in the country is carried off his feet by such a wave of bewilderment as to be led to include in his very sympathetic notice a statement like that I have quoted ?   And this critic was not alone.

My own guess is that what is worrying people is not absence of " law " in the *form* of the work, but the application of Scriabin's own self-made laws in the *harmony*.   I believe we all of us are in danger of losing our heads when we experience the shock of new harmonies.   Such subjects as the following (to quote the opening of two of the principal subjects of the piece we are discussing) are perfectly normal in everything but their harmonies—granted, of course, that these affect the intervals of the melodies also (though not their general curves) :

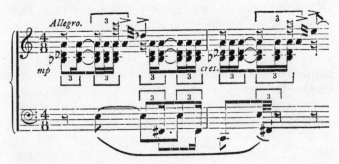

Right through the history of music this question of the acceptance of new harmonies has been a bugbear. From the period (not so many centuries ago) when it was first discovered that anything beyond unisonous music was possible, the development of harmonic resources has gone forward. At one time mere bare 5ths, 8ves, and 4ths were used, then 3rds were added, then 7ths, then 9ths—and so on. A distinction has always been recognized between restful chords (or " concords ") and unrestful chords (or " discords "). On the occasion of a recent Scriabin recital by our other active Scriabin player, Miss Lillias Mackinnon, a quite model programme book was provided by Mr. Edwin Evans, who in his introduction put this matter of Scriabin's harmonic innovation, as I think, very clearly :

In the most often cited example a succession of superimposed fourths leads to a chord which Scriabin deliberately accepts as a consonance. This he is logically entitled to, as the return from his furthest dissonance to this point of repose covers harmonically a greater distance than the resolution of discord into concord that is the basis of our music. It can at most be questioned whether he has not robbed himself by discarding that portion of the harmonic palette which lies between his point of repose and that commonly accepted. It is open to a painter to call cream-colour white and key his sharper tones accordingly, but in doing so he lessens his resources by the tones which exist between cream-colour and Chinese white.

One more point about " advanced " piano harmonies. They are much easier to bear in soft passages than in loud, and, I think, in slow passages than in quick. But a good deal seems to depend on the player, who needs to " settle down " to the piece before he gets the right relations of the dynamics of chords (and perhaps, in some cases, of the different notes of a single chord). This seems to be a process of unconscious adjustment. I remember putting the then newly published Ireland Sonata before a certain player who can play you any mortal thing correctly at first sight, and agreeing with him that some of the harmonies sounded rather brutal. Next day I heard Lamond give the same work its first public performance, and felt no shock at any single chord in the piece. Partly, this might be due to my having taken off the edge of the harmonic novelty by the previous day's hearing, and by study of the score, but I believe that a great part of the explanation was that Lamond, having practised the piece, had " worked himself into it," and, probably without knowing it, discovered the true dynamic values. A similar matter is, perhaps, not so easy to explain. Why did Scriabin's *forte* and *fortissimo* muted brass effects sound so shockingly ugly when we first began to make acquaintance with his orchestral works, and why do they now begin to sound so natural ? Experiences like this should warn us against too ready intellectual acquiescence in our early sensory impressions. There are times when to sit on the fence is the only honest thing to do.

Before leaving this subject, let me allude briefly to what appears to me a very strange fact. Scriabin's old friends, who heard his works from his own fingers before they were published, and who then helped to popularize them in Russia and elsewhere, come to this country and play us little or nothing of his.   Hofmann, who has once or twice lately been here, was one of the first to play Scriabin's works, was for a time in close personal touch with the composer, and was greatly admired by him.   Siloti is another old friend and colleague.   Kussevitsky, who from time to time visits London, had intimate relations with Scriabin, as publisher of some of his works and as conductor of many of them at Moscow and Petrograd and else-where.   Any of these three might give us a complete Scriabin programme, and, I think, have the hall packed.   It is more than probable that Scriabin quar-relled with each of them before his death (as far as I can gather, he did so with everybody).   But one cannot imagine that that is what stands in the way. It is our loss artistically (and, despite the disappear-ance of the " novelty-interest " in Scriabin, I think, theirs financially) that they neglect to give us the advantage of their first-hand acquaintance with the authentic Scriabin tradition.

IV. SCRIABIN AS PIANIST

There must be a good many amongst my readers who heard Scriabin's two London recitals of 1914, and who retain a pretty clear recollection of his playing. These may care to compare with their own impressions some taken from the Russian source I mentioned, and to others (especially any who are them-selves pianists and accustomed to perform Scriabin's works) the description I shall give may be of quite as great interest.

Scriabin's piano teacher, Safonof, was never tired of praising his playing. Scriabin had, he tells us, " a supreme grasp of a fact which is so important to pianists, and which I have always instilled into my pupils—the fact that the less a piano under the fingers of a performer resembles a piano, the better it is." This is a statement that, taken by itself, could easily be misinterpreted by an unimaginative and literal-minded person, but the idea becomes fairly clear from the context. " Much in his style of playing was his. And peculiar to himself were his variety of tone and his ideally refined use of the pedal; he possessed a rare and exceptional gift—with him the instrument *breathed*!" Often Safonof would draw the attention of the whole class to Scriabin's pedalling, telling them not to look at his hands, but at his feet. " Like Sasha's pedalling," was Safonof's highest compliment to a pupil. (" Sasha "—diminutive for Alexander.)

We can get a little clearer idea of Scriabin's view of the pianist as artist by recalling a few of his remarks in later years to his own pupils. (It will be recalled that for six years or so of his early manhood he held a post as professor of piano at his *alma mater*, the Moscow Conservatory.) " No mere passages: it must all live!" he used to say. " A passage may even be smeared, but if it's finished brilliantly you get an impression of clearness as well as brilliancy." This recalls Macdowell's remark to a pupil when he brought to him his own " Sonata Tragica." On the third page of the slow movement of this are certain passages that technically are scales. Macdowell (so his wife, herself a pianist, relates) turned to the boy and said :

" Of course, you must be able to play those runs clearly, absolutely so, but they must not sound like scales, but like a *sweep of colour*, such as a painter might make with a brush." In other words, as Mrs. Macdowell comments, " the runs should not be obscure and cloudy through faulty technique, but from intention." Others of Scriabin's *dicta* were : " Just like breathing " ; " Art must transfigure life " ; " Rapture before everything else " ; " Il faut se griser " ; " Pay no attention to criticism. Don't let it exist for you, but do what you ought to do " ; " Fear the trivialities of life. First and foremost the atmosphere of art." Some of these ejaculations, baldly repeated, seem fairly trite, but they are the kind of thing a too soberly conscientious pupil needs to stir him to a proper degree of self-forgetfulness. From a player, we are told, Scriabin required first of all " soul, a nervous uplifting." " Even the technique he drilled into his pupils may, in some respects, be called a technique of the nerves." His piano lessons must have proved a tonic to pupils who were capable of profiting by them ; others, one may guess, were little happier with their piano teacher than Scriabin had been with his own teacher of composition. Scriabin was not fond of teaching, and lacked some of the qualifications for it. When he came across a pupil who responded to his artistic ideas he was happy, and to such, in spite of his lack of system, he was a delightful and profitable teacher ; as a rule, however, his lessons were a torment to him—and hence, as we may perhaps guess, to those he taught.

Scriabin rarely used his own compositions when

teaching, and then only when pressed to do so by the pupil. He made his pupils play a good deal of Chopin and Liszt, and also Schumann, Bach's Fugues, Beethoven's Sonatas and the G major Concerto, Grieg's Concerto, Tschaikovsky's B flat minor Concerto, and so forth—in fact, quite the normal teaching repertoire. " Possibly he modernized Bach and Beethoven too much, but he made one love them anew." When he himself interpreted Beethoven, he imparted to the music such a tinge of his own brilliant individuality that you saw Scriabin in the foreground and Beethoven behind ; in this respect he differed greatly from his colleague, Medtner (also a pupil of Safonof), with whom you found Beethoven in the foreground and the performer well behind. Very occasionally Scriabin would give a " programme " of some favourite piece of music. Thus, on one occasion, he gave the following for Chopin's C sharp minor Etude (obviously the one in Op. 25, not the one in Op. 10)—" Evening ; someone sitting in his room alone and in anguish ; through the wide-open window comes the breath of the marvellous summer night (B major—here we have another feeling, everything is different) ; then the anguish again (C sharp minor)." But his performance of a work differed greatly on different occasions, and evidently that " technique of the nerves " meant leaving a good deal to the feeling of the moment.

In his own student days, Scriabin's toil at his instrument had been excessive. He had a great determination to outstrip all his fellow-students in technique. But one of these, I. Levin, had quite phenomenal virtuosity, and in trying to outdo him

Scriabin so concentrated on the diabolically difficult "Islamey" and Liszt's "Don Juan" Fantasia that he almost lost the use of his right hand for ever. The doctor told him the damage was done and was irreparable. Scriabin took on the treatment of his own case, improved his general health by a course of koumiss, gradually and persistently exercised the hand, and, at last, was able to use it as freely as ever. It was whilst this right hand was useless that Scriabin composed the well-known Prelude and Nocturne for left hand alone (Op. 9)—two quite gentle pieces and unoriginal, apart from their special intention, and pieces for both of which the normal player, not bent on astonishing, would use ten fingers rather than five, to the advantage of the performance. He also wrote for left hand alone a paraphrase of a Strauss Waltz, which he was often heard to play, but which may never have been written out, as it is not now to be found.

V. SCRIABIN AS A THINKER

Drawing still upon the document alluded to, I give some further particulars of Scriabin's ways of thought, such as, I believe, have not before been published in our language. I turn for the moment to the subject of Scriabin's attitude towards books, because what I have to relate on this subject has a very distinct bearing upon an important question as to the amount of importance we should attach to the philosophic "programmes" underlying many of his works. I think it is evident that we should not be too ready to take Scriabin as philosopher too seriously. He was

intensely interested in philosophical discussion, and
the philosophical ideas that teemed in his brain were
a great source of inspiration ; but those ideas were
not the result of hard study and clear thought. His
mind was agile but not laborious.

The First Symphony, written at the age of twenty-
three, is regarded by my Russian authority as showing
the " first attempt to connect sound with thought,
music with philosophy and religion." Pianist readers
will place this with rough accuracy if I say that it
follows the Third Sonata and the Nine Mazurkas.
The Third Sonata is considered by Gunst as marking
the last moment of spiritual affinity with Chopin, but,
as Mr. Montagu-Nathan has pointed out, there is just
as good ground for considering it rather as the first-
fruits of the composer's emancipation. Nine years
after its composition Scriabin took the occasion of a
recital in Brussels to circulate a prose-poem description
of the psychological content of the Sonata. Just
where we shall find the " first attempt to connect
sound with thought, music with philosophy," is, then,
doubtful—probably in the Sonata rather than in the
Symphony, but attempts to be precise on such a
matter are valueless, because a man's mental growth
is a slope and not a flight of steps. What is clear is
that, quite early in his career, Scriabin had become
involved in a habit of philosophizing and of expressing
in tone the resultant emotions. My authority goes
on : " From his youth he had been interested in
broad, general, philosophic ideas, which he worked
out for himself ; he did not adopt those of other men.
He never liked studying books systematically ; a

thought gleaned from a glance through a book, an observation made by a companion—these were enough to set his mind to work. When reading a book he very quickly grasped the essential idea (the details did not interest him), and he developed it in his own way, with the result that sometimes the ideas which he attributed to other men were really his own, whilst ideas which he considered his own were really those of others."

In another part of my document occurs an example of this sort of thing, which I will give in a moment. I am not sure whether there is such a thing as " orthodoxy " amongst Theosophists. The name itself would include a very wide range of thought, and I understand that no confession of faith is required of members of the Theosophical Society. But presumably there is a body of generally accepted doctrine, and I suppose the present-day source of this would be the writings of Scriabin's compatriot, Madame Blavatsky. Scriabin, at all events, made these works his study—if the word " study " can be used, for I learn that " in reading a page of Blavatsky he would seize upon something approaching to his own ideas and soar away with it to his own visionary heights." Boldly jumping into the middle of a new metaphor, the document goes on : " The freight that he carried under the flag of Blavatsky was not hers at all, but his own." At one time, I gather, Scriabin was very aggressive, and even pugnacious, in his philosophical views, and sometimes shocked friends who differed from him by the furious attacks he made upon them. Later, however, he conquered himself somewhat, and exhibited more self-restraint.

SOME VIEWS ON STRAVINSKY

I. The Rite—and the Wrong of It

MANY " Rite of Spring " performances have come and gone, and musical London still marvels. The thing grips. It has an extraordinary force about it. It is elemental. It has the directness of a Rodin. It reminds one of " Adam " or " Le Penseur," or, perhaps, " La Main de Dieu." I am not sure that it does not recall in some ways the " Victor Hugo "—not the bust, but the full length which the sculptor has left only half hewn out of its native rock. Here every true Stravinskist will throw down this volume with distress. This is not " romantic " music—not even rough-hewn romantic music ! Is it not ? I am not so sure. To steer clear both of the " abhorred teeth " of Scylla and the " horrid throat " of Charybdis needs good seamanship. And that is what these people are trying to do, they tell us. The classical logic and the romantic " rhetoric " are both, they say, to be shunned. On the whole, if they must approach one or the other of the dangers, they prefer the classic. Scylla robs you of but a part of your navigating force, whereas Charybdis sucks down your whole ship.

Very roughly speaking, the Classical means the balanced and the logical. It puts form before feeling,

whereas the Romantic puts feeling before form.   And
Stravinsky and his admirers may decry both form and
feeling as they will, but can never get rid of either.
The " balance " of the simpler classical forms reappears
in such a piece as the second of the Stravinsky " Three
Pieces for Clarinet," which is obviously in " simple
ternary form " (I imagine you can goad these people
to fury by attaching text-book labels to their hero's
works ; at all events let us try !).   Here is a *legato*
" first section," a much-broken " second section," and
the *legato* " first section " again, and, more or less, each
of the sections is " developed " out of a little germ, or
" motif," on the same fundamental principle as a bit
of Beethoven " development."   All that is wrong with
the piece from the point of view of a stern classicist
is that its material is not worth much to begin with and
that the development is rather poor—the melodic line,
for instance, never sweeping up boldly to a climax, but
(see page 122) making two or three shots at the same
high note and then falling back.   The method of the
piece is the classical method, but it is clumsily carried
out.   And similarly in this " Rite " (see page 32 of the
published score) you have sometimes the Beethovenian
procedure of taking a little theme of, say, two bars in
length, repeating it once or twice and then dividing
it, so that first one half and then the other may be
repeated at various pitches and with altered rhythms—
which is really a fair description of a good deal of the
" development " of Beethoven's symphonies.

The fact is that these old composing dodges *will* creep
in, and I suppose they do so because they are a psychological necessity.   Obviously there are but three

possible ways of treating musical material. Either (a) you can take the same little bit and repeat it to us over and over again (which is boresome, and, therefore, never done), or (b) you can give us one bit of new material, after another (which is mentally exhausting to the hearers, and, therefore, also never done), or (c) you can give us your first thought, pass by and by to a second, and then come back to your first, which root principle of form is that of most folk-tunes, a good many hymn tunes, all Bach, all Haydn, all Mozart, all Beethoven, all Wagner, all Franck, all Scriabin, and—all Stravinsky, or nearly all. And the abhorred " development " of Beethoven is but a method of carrying out this dual principle of diversity and repetition, or variety in unity. Where Stravinsky fails, formally that is, is in so often repeating his themes as they stand instead of with a multitude of little changes. He really thus gives us much less subtle Beethoven, Beethoven in the crude state. Mr. Diaghilev's little account some time ago of the remarks after his Paris performance, as an orchestral piece, of the " Rite " amused me rather. " But, said Mr. Salteena with surprise, surely this is Beethoven. No, said the Duke, it is Better." Still, as I have just shown, Mr. Diaghilev's friends were partly right ; there is a Beethovenishness to be found in Stravinsky ; it is, so to speak, Beethoven in half-solution, and when it crystallizes out again we do not know what it will be like. I should say its real novelty lies in its harmony, or rather, its deliberate " no-harmony," and in its post-impressionistic method of laying on the orchestral colour. Those are the two regions in which Stravinsky is most an explorer. In the ingenuity of

his combination of rhythms there is perhaps less innovation, but that is a quality in which he is phenomen-
ally strong.

As for the avoidance of Romanticism, I cannot help
saying that it seems to me that even the most balanced
of Stravinsky's admirers talk a good deal of nonsense.
We saw the original ballet of the " Rite " in 1913, and
it teemed with romantic ideas. It took our imagination back to the days of pre-historic nature-worship,
and soaked us in the spirit of Paganism, just as
" L'homme qui rit " takes us back to the underworld
of mountebank life and the upperworld of English
Society in the seventeenth century, or " Notre Dame "
to the scurrying human ant-hill of Paris in the sixteenth.
The effort was obviously made, by whatever means, to
pull us out of our stalls and boxes and plant us down
romantically on a sort of Russian Salisbury Plain, and
to awe us with the gloom and terror of human sacrifice, of primitive man tremblingly endeavouring to
propitiate and turn to his needs the sterner and kinder
forces of nature. For a critic to have said after the
Drury Lane performance in 1913, " No ! This is abstract music ; the Nijinsky choreography and the
Roerich décor are a mistake ; the piece is really a
Symphony," would have been to bring on himself the
crushing weight of argument and sarcasm of enraged
Stravinskists, Nijinskists, and Diaghilevians. Yet
that is what the Stravinskists themselves now tell us.
In the annotated programme of a recent performance
(the best-written annotated programme we have seen
for years, for the art of the annotated programme has
now fallen very low), Mr. Evans told us, " Though

commissioned as a ballet, ' Le Sacre du Printemps ' is
in all but name a modern symphony, and is therefore
to be regarded as abstract music, despite its original
purpose." Let Mr. Evans tell this tale to the distinguished musician (whoever he may be) who conducts
the band of the Horse Marines. No other musician
who either heard the work or read his own programme
to it will believe him.

Does Mr. Evans himself believe his assertion ?
Either he is trying to hoodwink us (which I do not
for a moment believe), or else he has deceived himself.
If, as he tells us, " the suggestion of a programme has
done more harm than good," why does he perpetuate
it, continuing (surely rather naïvely) : " Nevertheless,
for the purposes of guidance, the indications embodied
in the sectional titles provide a convenient nomenclature," and adding that they " will serve to describe
the progress of the music " ?   Surely if this nomenclature and these sectional titles are so misleading they
were better away.   It is difficult to listen to the " Rite "
as " the first abstract music ever written," as Mr.
Evans or somebody of his entourage has surely called
it, when he himself begins his description with such
words as " The subject, then, is Spring," and speaks
of the Prelude of Part Two as " gloomy with the
oppression of the vast forces of Nature, pitiful with the
helplessness of living creatures in their presence."   Of
course, he guards all this ; we are given " Spring from
within, Spring stripped bare of its literary associations," and the sadness is " physical, not sentimental "
(whatever that may mean).

I wonder, by the way, whether the Stravinsky-

Evans notion of " Spring stripped of its literary associations, and presented bare *sans phrases*," is within
the power of concept of the normal mind. Mine
struggles with it, but finds it slippery. And this idea
of " pure abstract sound," of " sonority itself exhaling
an emotion," which emotion " is the very essence of
abstract music "—what are we to say of that ? The
" Rite," we are told, is " full to bursting with emotion,
but the emotion is not poetic—it is purely musical."
Speaking at all strictly, is such snowy-white emotion
(or " feeling " ?) possible ? Are we capable of such a
feat as a pure musical feeling unconnected with associations ? Will the psychologists tell us ? I put the
point to one of them the other day, sitting over him
whilst he read Mr. Evans's article, and watching his
face closely. His reply, as I understood it, was in the
negative. " The nearest thing," he said, " to such a
feeling in music could only be experienced by a mind
used from habit or preference to specialize. So that a
musical appeal to pure feeling would only touch a small
group, and would therefore be bad socially. But
music written with the purpose of arousing this pure
feeling would not have the desired effect on the major-
ity of an audience, who would bring their own associations to it." As I have hinted, Mr. Evans himself
helped us to " bring associations to it " recently.
And, frankly, is not the " Rite " a piece of the most
closely written " programme music " ever composed,
and is not all this talk about its " absolute " and
" abstract " quality mere (unconscious) bluff ? Perhaps the time of my conversion will come, and if it
does I shall declare it, but for the moment I have no

more expectation of ever in my life experiencing the
artistic delights of Mr. Evans' " pure abstract sound "
than I have of being able to put my chair some day
under a big bell-jar in a physicist's laboratory and to
live for ten days in a vacuum.

Of course all this is not to say that the work is not
well worth listening to and closely studying. It is !
Get the score and look into it carefully. It is now
not only published for piano duet (with *primo* and
secondo parts placed over and under one another, not
on opposite pages, so that a good deal can be made out
from them) but as a " miniature " orchestral score. The
orchestration of the " Rite " is amazing. Sometimes
it is positively stunning, and I, for one, have more
than once come away from the Queen's Hall breathing out all the threatenings of the Athanasian Creed
and the Imprecatory Psalms against the individual in
the top row of the orchestra who, when all his fellows
of the percussion were already " doing their damned-
est," too often added to their diabolical din that of a
huge brass gong beaten with the full force of a heavy
wooden mallet. But understand that I wish you to
divest those ideas of the Athanasian Creed and the
Imprecatory Psalms of all their " literary associations," just as Mr. Evans tells you to do when he calls
a page of Stravinsky " Cercle Mystérieux des Adoles-
centes " or " Evocation des Ancêtres." The emotion
of my curses is a purely cursing emotion, and the
terms I have used are a mere " convenient nomenclature," a mere " indication," for " the purposes of
guidance." This " naked directness," however, of my
cursing emotion does not detract from its violence.

II. " HONEST DOUBT "

Can we get to the bottom of this strange theory that
" The Rite " is " in all but name a modern symphony,
and is, therefore, to be regarded as abstract music,
despite its original purpose " (the quotation is from
Mr. Evans's programme book to the Goossens performance) ? It is worth trying, because this seems to be
part of the ultra-modernist's official explanation of
every new work that puzzles us. (Even Holst's
" Planets," which hardly needs the defence, is spoken
of by Mr. Evans in similar terms—see the publisher's
leaflet advertising the score of this work.)   If we could
grasp the theory we should, I suppose, more quickly
understand the works, and so, perhaps, increase our
pleasures. To my last chapter, when it appeared as
a newspaper article, Mr. Evans duly published a reply.
As this is brief I wish, in fairness to him, to give it in
full. After discussing criticism the " Rite " had received in another quarter, he went on :

" We found more interest in the comments of Mr.
Percy Scholes as an honest doubter. But is he really
in doubt ?   At the very outset of his article he declares
that ' the thing grips,' that ' it has an extraordinary
force about it,' and ' the directness of a Rodin.' If
it has gripped him to this degree it has fulfilled its
purpose so far as he is concerned, and what more
does he ask of any music ? If it has the power to
grip a confessed honest doubter it is great music,
and that is what has been contended on its behalf.
Whether the composer has or has not given away
the key to his method is quite another question, and
irrelevant to the issue. But Mr. Scholes raises two

points which are of interest. He writes that if a critic of 1913 had said that ' Le Sacre ' is really a symphony he would have brought upon himself the crushing weight of argument and sarcasm of enraged Stravinskyists. It may surprise him to learn that this was the view which emerged from conversations which we had with the composer both before and after the initial performances of 1913, and to which we have adhered ever since, strongly deprecating the literal attribution of the music to an attempt at depicting the Stone Age. The other point relates to the annotated programme, and its use for purposes of nomenclature of the labels given in the only published edition. Circumstances at present are against the use of musical examples in programmes. These labels have the disadvantage, which was pointed out in the programme, of conveying unnecessary associations ; but if Mr. Scholes can point out a more convenient way of identifying the various sections without the help of musical illustrations we shall be interested to hear of it."

I will answer first the last point. The " more convenient way " that is desired is surely ready enough to hand ; for a century or so it has been customary to speak of the various sections of a " symphony " as " First Movement," " Second Movement," and so on. If one really does wish to avoid the dangerous entanglement of those objectionable " associations " which the composer himself has introduced by heading his sections by such titles as " Cortège du Sage," or " Danse Sacrale," or " Jeux des Cités Rivales," why not adopt this time-honoured method ? My suggestion is that, against what he would perhaps consider his better judgment, Mr. Evans, as official-programme-annotator-in-chief-to-the-ultra-moderns, is perpetuating these designations because, perhaps half-unconsciously, he recognizes that they are likely to help the listener. And if they help the listener it is because they describe the original purpose of each section. And if each section had a purpose that can be described in these picturesque terms the contention that the work " is to be regarded as abstract music " falls to the ground. But I must remind Mr. Evans of a good many points in my criticism of his description of the work to which he has not attempted to reply.   What, for instance, of the passage I quoted from him in which he described the Introduction to Part II. of the " Rite " as " gloomy with the oppression of the vast forces of Nature, piti- ful with the helplessness of living creatures in their presence " ?   This phrase, at any rate, is not a mere " indication " ;   it is a romantic description.   The words " Introduction to Part II." would be sufficient " indication," but, as a matter of fact, in addition to giving us this " programmatic " description of the movement, Mr. Evans has actually gone right out of his way to supply a title not given even in the pub- lished score—" La Nuit Païenne."

When I recently offered a word of praise of Mr. Evans' writing he publicly thanked me for a tribute from which, a week after, he was " still blushing," but told me that I had offered him " a bouquet with an asp concealed in it," for I had " called him an extrem- ist, and that stings."   Very well, then, Mr. Evans is *not* an extremist ; he is merely an honest believer, as I am an " honest doubter," and I will bring up against him a genuine " extremist," and one who would, I think, actually glory in the shameful name. Jean Cocteau, in his " Cock and Harlequin," describes " The Rite of Spring " in these words :

" Let us recall the theme of the ' Sacre.'

" FIRST TABLEAU. The prehistoric youth of Russia are engaged in springtide games and dances ; they worship the earth, and the wise elder reminds them of the sacred rites.

" SECOND TABLEAU. These simple men believe that the sacrifice of a young girl, chosen from amongst all her peers, is necessary in order that spring may recommence. She is left alone in the forest ; the ancestors come out of the shadows like bears, and form a circle. They inspire the chosen one with the rhythm of a long-drawn-out convulsion. When she falls dead the ancestors draw near, receive her body, and raise it towards heaven."

Now, obviously, if that is " the theme of the ' Sacre,' " the " Sacre " *has* (or had) a theme. And if it has (or had) a theme, it is not " abstract music," nor a " Symphony," but a piece of closely fitted ballet music, now, for some reason, deprived of its ballet. And a glance at the score bears this out. Take, for instance, what Mr. Evans and Stravinsky himself call " Les Augures Printaniers," but should properly, according to their theory, call merely " Second Movement." If you have not got the score, go to the piano and play in four-time any two chance handfuls of notes low down on the piano, varying the accent from bar to bar. You will then have, as I think, a fairly reasonable reproduction of the main musical (or unmusical) material of this

movement. Now my recollection is that in the original
ballet this was the instrumental accompaniment to a
stamping motion by a gang of heavy-footed pre-his-
torians, who, with bent bodies and eyes glassy with
religious concentration, were trying, by treading it
down, to promote the fertility of the earth (personally
I should prefer to reverse the process and use a spade).
In my simple-minded 1913 ignorance of this music's
being abstractedly symphonic, I took that musical
theme to be definitely devised as the most expressive
possible accompaniment to this particular action, and
when I am told that in the concert-room I am to forget
all about that action and enjoy the movement as a
piece of " pure " music, I am compelled to turn round
and tell the programme writer that in his efforts to
help my enjoyment he has really hindered it, and,
indeed, I fear, robbed me of my only chance of seeing
any sense in future in the scraping and blowing and
banging and clattering of Mr. Goossens's wonderful
hundred-and-five picked orchestral players as they
perform the work. Is this passage pure music?
Never in this world! The theory which is now attached to it cannot, in any case, be very " pure "—
for it certainly won't wash!

My belief is that in all these elaborate explanations
we hear the naïve protestations of tail-less foxes. I
am capable even of rudely suggesting that the explanation of the preference of the composer for endless
repetitions of phrases, rather than logical development
of them, is due to the fact that these were originally
designed as the modest accompaniment of repeated
actions of arms and legs, and then, taken apart from

their actions, had to be justified by a new theory of composition, which is henceforth to be the basis of a new " school." In any case, if, as is now hinted, the composer himself " deprecated," even in 1913, the idea that he was attempting to " depict the Stone Age " (by which we none of us, I hope, mean that he is charged with attempting to suggest the music of the Stone Age) then he was unfaithful to his colleagues, Diaghilev, Nijinsky, and Roerich. He was asked to write them some ballet music to fit certain movements and ingeniously foisted on them a " pure " symphony—? I don't think !

I must say, frankly, that I am bewildered by some of Stravinsky's recent proceedings. Why cannot he decide when he first writes a work what it is to be ? He wrote the " Rite " as a Ballet Drama and then produced it as a Symphony—*and not a note changed !* He wrote the " Nightingale " as an Opera, and then turned it into a Ballet. " Renard," in the score in my possession, is an Opera, but it has, I believe, been produced under its composer's own direction as a Ballet. I take it that the Nightingale and the Fox are on a journey ; they began together in the country of Opera and have both now reached the realm of Ballet, and in a year or so will arrive safely in the haven of Symphony. This is a touching pilgrimage in search of " purity." But, unless they really change their natures en route, we shall find them at the end the same old bird and beast, and they will be no more " pure " than they were when they first set out.

Mr. Evans has, as I gently complained above, by no means answered all my objections, but I wish to answer

all his. One remains. If I am "gripped" by the
"Rite," "what more do I ask of any music?" To
which the easy reply is that I might find myself
"gripped" by a ju-jitsuist, or a member of Mr. de
Valera's forces (if they still exist), or a Chinese bandit,
or one of the "Apaches" of Mr. Evans' beloved Paris—
and yet not be immediately and completely convinced
of his extreme personal attractions.

III. STRAVINSKY IN THE NURSERY

There will be tears in the schoolroom over this!
But Phyllis, having had her knuckles rapped, will protest tearfully, "But, Miss Brown, it *is* F sharp!"
And the governess, peering carefully into the music,
will have to admit herself in the wrong and will say,
resignedly, that if the great and good Mr. Stravinsky
says "F sharp," F sharp she supposes it must be.

For Stravinsky is now in the nursery—or soon will
be! He has actually written a book of five-finger
exercises, not of the dull Schmitt kind, that gives you
just a bar of quavers and instructs you to repeat it
world without end, but short studies of a page or so
each, "eight finely contrasted pieces," say his publishers (who should know), "pieces that fully reveal his
personality." So here we are, at last, with the opportunity of studying Stravinsky's personality at short
range. Many of my readers have heard the "Rite,"
some of them may have bought the piano duet score of
it, and may have practised with a companion, or (I
find this the better way, since it avoids recriminations
between the struggling performers) have pedalled it out

on their pianolas from the excellent rolls of the Æolian
Company ; still others may have studied it from the
recently issued miniature orchestral score.   But there
must be some who cannot play the " Rite " by hand,
have no pianola, and are unable to read a full orchestral
score, and who will be glad to get hold of " Les Cinq
Doigts—Eight Very Easy Pieces on Five Notes "
(Chester, 3s.), and to study the Stravinsky idiom from
that.   I commend this spirit of earnest inquiry, and
trust that nothing I am about to say will check it.
Get " Les Cinq Doigts," and judge of its musical and
educational value for yourselves.

At the outset you will, I think, be struck by a curious
technical detail.   " Eight Very Easy Pieces on Five
Notes," says the title-page, but at a glance you will see
that the five-note principle is only observed in the right
hand.   At the beginning of each piece the composer,
with the most fatherly care, tells the child where to
place that hand, by a little diagram :

But whilst the right-hand part faithfully follows the
diagram, the left-hand part jumps all over the place :

I do not understand the idea.   At first glance I thought
the pieces were for exceptional children with five fin-

gers on one hand and eight or nine on the other, but
then, catching sight of our educationally-minded composer's so thoughtfully provided fingering for the left-
hand part, I saw that this was not so.   My next idea
was that they were for children whose right hand was
six years old and whose left hand was twelve years old.
But then I read again the publisher's note, " within the
compass of five notes to *each hand* [my italics] *played
without change of position*," and saw that what had happened was a mere detail of oversight.   It seems, however, to be a rather important detail, does it not ?
Can you quite see the child who needs a tiny stretch
and such ease of passage work in the right hand com-
passing in the left hand these bigger stretches and held
notes (with the weak little finger, too) ?—

But, after all, those are professional questions for Miss
Brown to answer, as is also that as to whether the five-
note child will be able to grapple with some of the
rhythmic problems :

But, though we leave poor Miss Brown to settle these practical problems, are we not entitled to wonder quietly whether the mind that set her them is one which works quite normally—like yours and mine, for instance ? We admit that Stravinsky is diabolically clever, that, right up to his middle period, he has written things which we must all admire, that he is, in several respects, a most courageous pioneer. But what about his reasoning power ? I have earlier questioned the validity of some of the arguments of Stravinsky and the Stravinskists that seemed to me to have flaws and gaps, and I think this new volume confirms my idea that we are not, in them, to look for logic or straight-line discussion. Stravinsky works by impulse and instinct—which I freely admit may, in many cases, be the better guide to an artist. You cannot have everything in one man, and here you see that the brain which can conceive the " Rite of Spring " or the " Symphony of Wind Instruments " is incapable of thinking out what can be done and what cannot be done in writing a child's five-finger exercise. This does not impair the value of the " Rite " or the " Symphony," but it does impair the explanations of them that have been given us. Those of us who can see little beauty in the one work and none at all in the other may, in old age, come to admit with shame that we were deaf, and wish that we'd been dumb. But we are little likely to come to admit that the theorizing by and of Stravinsky to which we have sometimes listened was also sound.

But, whatever their value to the nursery, these exercises may be of value to us. Here is Stravinsky

reduced to his lowest terms.   Can we work out from
these pages his system of harmony ?   Obviously,
chords to him mean something different from what they
mean to me.   What do they mean to him ?   Then
what is his idea of rhythm ?   Rhythmically, I feel
the following, for instance, to be very lame (I allude
especially to the cadence phrase and its final bump).
But it means something to Stravinsky.   What ?

POLYTONALITY AND ATONALITY

I. Polytonality

THERE must be a good many people who are still asking themselves " Whence and Whither ? " They are aware of the need for patience with " modern music." They know they cannot at once hope to grasp the whole purport of music fashioned upon a new system (and for many " The Rite " is still that), but, as every new style recorded in the history of music has grown out of an earlier one, and led to a later one, they would like some convinced modernist to explain to them his ancestry and forecast his posterity, for the experience of apparently unrelated phenomena is always disturbing. After their failure to make themselves clear on the æsthetic side, on which I have already commented, can the modernists at least make themselves clear on the technical ? Well, Milhaud, in an article, " Polytonalité et Atonalité," in a recent issue of the admirable " Revue Musicale " (3, Rue de Grenelle, Paris VIe.), succeeds in giving a pretty plain exposition of two phases of the " modernist " harmony, showing how they have evolved by perfectly logical processes out of the previously accepted system, and hinting, at the end of his article, at the nature of the further growth which is inevitable. He classes modernist harmony under two heads, " Polytonality," or simultaneous use of different keys, and " Atonality," or entire absence of key. I here summarize briefly his treatment of the one phase, and will do the same in my next chapter for his treatment of the other.

The harmony in which we were brought up was for the most part diatonic, that is to say, the notes making up a chord, or the " parts " woven together into a contrapuntal fabric, all belonged to a definite (major or minor) key, and of keys there were twenty-four (twelve major and twelve minor). Necessarily, however, the music passed, from time to time, from one key into another. The admission that succession of key, or " modulation," was acceptable inevitably implied, says Milhaud, that, at some later stage, superposition of key (" Polytonality ") would also be found equally acceptable. This hardly seems to follow, but the writer has omitted a stage in the argument, of a hint as to which I will make him a present. For thousands of years only unisonous (and octave) singing was tolerated, i.e., only succession of notes ; then, at last, the practice of harmonic singing grew up, i.e., superposition of notes. Apply this, by analogy, and the missing link in the argument is, I think, supplied. Since, a thousand years ago, we began to pass from Homophony to Polyphony and accomplished the process successfully, there seems no reason why we should not similarly pass from Homotonality to Polytonality.

An astute suggestion is made by Milhaud to the

effect that the device of " canon " sometimes pointed
to a polytonal future for music. Here, for instance,
is the opening of a Bach strict canon, at the interval
of the fourth :

Read the upper part of this without reference to the
lower ; it is in the key of D minor—modulating to
G minor and A minor (its Subdominant and Dominant).   Read the lower part without reference to the
upper ;   it is in A minor, modulating to D minor
and E minor (*its* Subdominant and Dominant).
There, then (when the piece is *contrapuntally considered*), is a specimen of Polytonality—with Bach
appearing as an eighteenth-century Milhaud-modern-
ist. Now read the two parts together and see how
Bach has, as a matter of fact (the piece being *harmonically considered*), skilfully evaded Polytonality,
his lower part supplying harmonies to the upper,
somewhat different from what one, at first sight of

the former, felt to be the natural ones, harmonies in which both parts can share, in a reasonable spirit of give and take, without parting company into different keys. This, then, is in one sense Polytonality avoided rather than accepted ; or, as one may say, listened to strictly horizontally, the piece is polytonal ; listened to perpendicularly, it is monotonal.

What are called appoggiaturas, accented passing notes and suspensions, supply Milhaud with another argument, pretty obvious and by no means unfamiliar. At one period in history ears would only stand unison-singing, or, as an Irishman might say, one-note chords ; next they tolerated two- and three-note chords, consisting of the simplest and most natural intervals (the third and the fifth) ; then they began to tolerate certain four-note chords (such, for instance, as the dominant seventh or certain " suspensions "). So far, all the notes of a chord had been in the one key, but soon it became common to insert in a chord a note borrowed from another key, provided it quickly merged into its " resolution." Cut out the resolution and you have Stravinskyism, Satieism, Milhaudism— all of which, a purist might say, enforces the Sunday-school lesson of the danger of small steps in the wrong direction. Our dilemma is that if we decide to follow this purist we shall, to be logical, have to make an effort to thrust ourselves back into fifth-century unisonous singing, or, indeed, into (literally) monotonous chant ; whilst, on the other hand, if we elect to act upon the Milhaud theory, we must, equally logically, in time pass into a condition where anything is possible, almost the position, by the way, where he wishes us to be, as illustrated by this example of his own writing:

Other arguments I can only briefly mention. They are drawn from (*a*) the device of pedal, with modulations above it, as found commonly in the classics; (*b*) chords such as that of the ninth, eleventh, and thirteenth (here Milhaud, without knowing it, adopts the old " Day theory," in which some of us who used Macfarren's Harmony were brought up—i.e., he considers such chords as being combinations of two

different chords). And so on. It is all very alarming, as strict logic often is. But dare we say " Down
with logic " ? Up to the present there is seen to have
been a very strict logic governing the development
of music, and it is probable that we cannot escape it.

II. ATONALITY

In the previous chapter I briefly discussed Milhaud's
argument, based upon historical precedent, as to the
propriety of Polytonality (or simultaneity of key), a
principle which governs the harmonic structure of a
good deal of music to-day. I need hardly say that
no argument, however logical, can justify a piece of
music ; the music has to justify itself, but if the argument is sound it should have the effect of inducing
us to exercise greater patience than we might otherwise have done, and so to give the music a chance of
making its own appeal. To a musician who has
several times heard Ravel's Sonata for Violin and
'Cello, the Sonata probably becomes, in itself, an argument in favour of Polytonality, but until he has heard
it several times it is quite possible that he may need
to apply some logical argument about Polytonality in
favour of the Sonata. History shows that composers
do not as a rule first theorize as to harmonic systems,
and then carry out their theories ; rather they subconsciously feel their way towards new harmonic
systems and then go on to discovery of the principles
of these. That is precisely what is now occurring in
the case of Polytonality and Atonality ; they are
systems already in active being, and the process of

explanation and theoretical justification, which began
some years since, is now working itself out pretty
clearly. There will be written reams of thoroughly
bad Polytonic and Atonic music, as there have been
written reams of thoroughly bad Diatonic music.
What we are interested in for the moment is not the
value of the music but the soundness of the system.
But in listening to the music, to-morrow or next day,
it should be the other way about.

Having shown how Polytonality grew out of Homotonality by a perfectly natural evolution (canon, accented passing notes, pedals, etc.), Milhaud proceeds
to show us how Atonality is already growing out of
Polytonality. The argument is, briefly, this. Two
or more perfectly regular diatonic melodies super-
posed, each going its way regardless of the other, produce a harmonic effect of Polytonality ; horizontally
considered, the music is Diatonic, perpendicularly
considered, it is rarely so. Some few of the chords
produced by the coincidence of the notes of these
diatonic melodies may also, by accident, be normal
diatonic chords, assignable to one key or another,
and when this happens the effect is momentarily
diatonic, otherwise the result is chromatic. The
diatonic is the accident, the chromatic the rule, and
Polytonality is thus harmonically a chromatic system.
Presumably, if our ears were sufficiently trained to
the appreciation of the effects, we should feel the two
systems in use at one time, the one in each separate
part, the other in their combination, and this is probably what happens with a genuine polytonic composer ; indeed, to him the pleasure of his music pro-

bably consists largely in the agreeable conflict thus
introduced. Obviously the kind of listening required
is an extension of the kind of listening required for
the appreciation of a Byrd madrigal or a Bach fugue
—the perception, so to speak, of warp and woof at
one glance. Now, chromaticism knows no key. The
series D, D sharp, E, F, F sharp, for instance, is no
more in any one key than in any other, whether it
be used melodically or harmonically, and a good deal
of Polytonality being harmonically chromatic, it is
a small step deliberately to make the separate parts
or voices or strands also chromatic, taking our separate
melodies or parts from the keyless system. This
done, we have something like a complete Atonality,
or absence of key, the only reservation being that
even now, by pure accident (or the merciful hand of
Providence) a combination here or there may be a
recognizable " chord " of the old system, though,
even in this case, two such chords, assignable to the
same key, are little likely to occur in sequence, so
that no key effect is set up, and we have complete
Atonality.

For the practice of Polytonality, Milhaud gives
simple but ingenious tables showing the combinations
possible. Superposing all other possible major chords
upon that of C major, we have obviously eleven combinations. Superposing all possible minor chords on
it we have eleven more. Superposing all the major
chords on the chord of C minor we have another set
of eleven, and superposing all the minor chords upon
it still another set. This makes forty-four Polytonic
chords upon the one note C. As the same process

can be repeated over C sharp, D, etc., the forty-four can be multiplied by eleven = 484. Then come in the " inversions " of all these chords, but already I tire of arithmetic, whilst when it comes to the combinations possible by superposition of three chords of four (and these not necessarily simple " common chords," but also chords of the seventh, ninth, eleventh, thirteenth, etc.), I " reel to and fro, and stagger like a drunken man and am at my wit's end." And if all this is done in the green wood of Polytonality what shall be done in the dry of Atonality ? Presumably a senior wrangler would make short work of the little sum called for, but its prospect leaves me staring wild-eyed into infinity.

Then comes the troubling question (and Milhaud never really faces it)—Will all this variety of resource give us, in practice, greater variety of effect ? For the ear, to enjoy, has to classify ; classification is, with the ordinary listener, subconscious, of course, but none the less it goes on. Then, of course, one not only classifies single chords, feeling them as major, minor, diminished, etc., but " progressions " of two chords as dominant to tonic, tonic to sub-dominant, major to minor, and minor to major, and so forth. Is any such classification possible to our ears under the limitless new dispensation, and if not, shall we not simply experience a vague nondescript effect, one " chord " being very like another, and one progression like another ? What will be the composer's own method of selection of his effects ?

Then how, in the wonderful days that are coming, will students in composition be trained ? It is all

very well for Milhaud to talk airily of " complementary studies " :

Polytonality and Atonality are not arbitrary systems.
They are, the one a development from diatonic harmony and counterpoint, the other a development
from chromatic harmony and counterpoint, and ought
to be made the object of complementary technical
studies.

How are these studies to be carried out ? All that
he proposes is obviously lawful. But when, from
precedent to precedent the bounds of freedom have
been broadened down to this extent, anyone can do
anything, and nobody can say him nay. Which is
all very right and proper, but art necessarily implying
selection, a principle for the selection will have to be
first felt and next discovered. Milhaud seems to
imply a safeguard in a sort of *canto fermo* system :

The factor which will determine the Polytonic or
Atonic character of a work will be much less the
process of its composition [" le procédé d'écriture "
—I don't quite follow] than the essential melody
which will come from the " heart " alone of the
musician. It is the absolute and organic necessity
of the initial melody which will prevent the progressions (" procédés ") from congealing into a system
otherwise still-born. The whole life of a work will
depend upon nothing else than the melodic invention
of its composer, and Polytonality and Atonality will
do nothing more than furnish him with a vaster field,
richer means of composition, a more expressive and
complex scale, wherewith to employ his sensibility,
his imagination, and his fancy.

All very fine and large—especially the latter ! And, after this, what next ? Why, of course, a quarter-tone system, composition in which has already begun. And, after that—well, let us hope the resources here laid out for use will last our lifetime. Posterity must look out for itself !

COLOUR AND SOUND

THERE seems to be a surprising amount of dust flying about as a result of the first (public) London performance the other day of the " Colour Symphony " of Arthur Bliss, and I propose to lay some of it with the watering-can of plain fact. One sort of confusion that has occurred may be illustrated by two extracts from recent Press references to the work. In the " Daily Telegraph " recently a writer alluded to it in these terms : " Arthur Bliss's so-called (though I believe not by the composer) ' Colour Symphony,' " and in the " Saturday Review " of the same day an article, signed by D. H., opened : " It was unfortunate that Mr. Bliss allowed himself to be persuaded by Mr. Scholes into giving his ' Colour Symphony ' that title." To settle all personal questions once for all, I would say that Mr. Bliss is himself entirely responsible for the title chosen, my part having been merely to urge him, if he had any extra-musical idea in his mind when composing the work, to allow it to appear in the title, since such a description, as " in A flat, Op. 55," means nothing to the ordinary listener, not suggesting individuality, as does the name of a ship or a racehorse, but being a mere means of official reference, like the numbering of a car or a convict. As Mr. Bliss when composing has, as he then first informed me, a constant play of colour in his mind, and as each movement of this symphony was to him representative of a particular predominating colour, with a number of related colours or shades, it was natural that he should at once decide to call the work " A Colour Symphony," and to indicate the colour relations (with their symbolical significance) of each of its separate movements, a procedure which I see no reason for him to regret.

Coming to the more interesting and general question of colour associations with music, I may admit that I personally possess few, though I recalled with a start the other day that forty years ago I was not so stolidly unimaginative, for it was a frequent game with a younger brother and myself, before we were out of petticoats, as it may possibly have been with other children, to make " oos " and " ahs," high and low, loud and soft, and to cry, " that's a blue sound," or " that's a red sound." On the supposition that we were in those days still " trailing clouds of glory," it may be supposed that there is celestial sanction for our association, to the support of which theory I contribute the reminder that many of us, even in elder years, look upon harp tone as silvery and trumpet tone as bright orange or red. And science is, to some extent, on the side of the angels, admitting at least this much, that the spectrum band resembles the octave in music, the speed of light vibrations at the violet end being approximately double that of the speed at the red end, just as the speed of sound vibration of a higher C is double that of the C an octave lower.

It is evident, then, that a colour scale can be constructed with some close resemblance to the musical scale. Indeed, such a scale may be seen set forth in one of the plates of the late Professor Rimington's " Colour Music—the Art of Mobile Colour," where the suggested twelve semitones of the octave of colour are shown immediately above the twelve semitones of a musical octave, making it possible to play " colour symphonies " in real sooth upon a very ingenious " colour organ " devised by the author for the purpose, the change of lights upon a screen engaging the spectator's eye, either independently or at the same time as his ears are engaged by corresponding sounds simultaneously played upon the organ. Rimington maintained (as his sub-title suggests) that a missing art should be supplied, that of colour movement (apart from shape), and he argues that the practice of this art might restore to us the finer colour sense which our ancestors possessed in the days of gay clothing and of stained glass of a brilliance such as is now never produced. The East, said this author, still retains the colour sense which we have largely lost, and his plea for more attention to the subject is supported in a preface by Herkomer, who looked upon the colour organ as a valuable stimulus for the painter, imagining him seated at the keyboard and improvising slow and rapid, gradual and violent, colour changes, as a musician at the piano wanders over the keys, experimenting in harmonies. A note by Dr. Brown, of King's College, argues that " the scheme of introducing rhythm (i.e., the time relation) into colour combinations opens up an entirely new field of investigation of which psychologists will not be slow to avail themselves." That was written

ten years ago, and how far the psychologists have since carried the matter I do not know.

The spectrum-octave as the basis of relation seems to be temporarily abandoned by Rimington in the following passage, where, rather curiously, he substitutes for it that relation of timbres which means more to many of us :

We will suppose for the moment an orchestral composition as being accompanied by colour. Let us assume that the composition opens with a Wagnerian trumpet blast. The screen is at the same moment flooded by an intense orange, which palpitates with the harmonic colours corresponding to a subordinate passage upon some of the orchestral instruments. The blast ceases, there is a faint echo of it upon the violins while the screen pulsates with pale lemon and saffron, hardly discernible. Again comes the blare of trumpets, and once more the screen flares with orange.

The idea of performance here seems to be very like that of Scriabin in his " Prometheus," the score of which includes a stave for " Clavier à lumières." The changes and rhythms notated are not rapid or involved, rarely rising even to such complexities as this (I give the flute part underneath, so as to show a connection with the musical part of the score) :

It is impossible in a short essay seriously to discuss the subject of the relation of colours and sounds, but as against the theory of a definite connection between tonalities and colours I would point out that of musicians with a mental colour-tonality relation no two are agreed. The fact is, I think, that music can arouse emotions and that colours can do the same, and that what connection there is between music and colour is not physical and direct, but subjective and viâ emotion. This does not apply to key (except in the case where key has for a particular observer a fanciful emotional significance of its own). But it does apply to timbre and also to the general character of a passage (rhythm probably often entering as a factor). A trumpet fanfare suggests joy ; red to me suggests joy ; hence a trumpet fanfare to me suggests red. That is my idea of the matter !

THE MIND MADE UP

THERE was once a gentleman who rose in Parliament and said :

He craved the indulgence of the House for a few observations which he had to make. When he got up in the morning, and when he lay down at night, he always felt for the Constitution. On this question he had never had but one opinion. When he came first into Parliament, he remembered that the Chancellor of the Exchequer proposed a Reform, but he saw it was wrong and he opposed it. Would it not be madness to change what had been handed, sound and entire, down from the days of their fathers ?

There were, as you see, Die-Hards in the eighteenth century. This one was Sir Gregory Page-Turner, and you may check the accuracy of my quotation by turning up " Parliamentary Debates," May 26, 1797. The attitude taken seems extraordinary in a man sent to the place in which he spoke for the very purpose of amending the laws of his country, but it has its occasional counterpart in musical criticism.

In a British court of law the previous records are not to be read until, in the particular matter under trial, the prisoner's innocence or guilt has been established. This sound principle should, I am sure, direct us also in

173

musical criticism. It may be difficult to achieve the fine detachment of the ever-open mind, but it should be attempted. I have more than once seen the suggestion that some critic was evidently culpably wrong in some instance mentioned, since he had gone against accepted judgments, and adversely commented upon accepted classics. But surely the critic who went to a concert intimidated by phrases such as " accepted judgments " and " accepted classics " would be, in reality, no critic. He would be in the same dishonest position as a critic who went to a concert determined to welcome all novelty and modernity, and how would our objectors like that ? It is the very foundation of sound critical practice to put aside prepossession and to judge each composer and each composition (" classical " or " modern "), each performer and each performance (of established artist or of new-comer) as though one had never heard the names before. All appraisement not based on this principle of absolute open-mindedness is useless and even dangerous. And here let me say that when I speak of " criticism " and " appraisement," I am not alluding merely to the work of those who undertake those duties as stipendiaries. In this court all are judges, and one of the most unyielding barriers to musical progress in this country to-day is the glaring indifference to its judicial duties of the general concert-going public.

I think it may be remembered by some that, when it seemed called for, I have been somewhat downright in the exposure of what I felt to be unwarranted pretensions on the part of some of the " modernist " composers and their protectors. I am therefore marked out by duty as the one who should also make a protest against the undue influence of the dead hand of the past. " Would it not be madness to change what had been handed, sound and entire, down from the days of our fathers ? " are almost the words in which some attack all criticism of (for instance) Beethoven. Beethoven, I think, does not value blind and deaf worship of this sort : the works of Beethoven call for sifting, like those of any other composer, ancient or modern, and he knows he will gloriously survive the process. The unthinking assumption of large numbers of people is that all Beethoven is great, and this necessarily brings bewilderment on the part of less experienced and more simpleminded people who hear some particular piece of Beethoven and feel it to be lacking in any quality of greatness, and a definite reaction on the part of a small number of rebellious spirits—a reaction that will soon spread if the Die-Hards persist in stimulating it.

The position of Beethoven to-day is, I believe, somewhat like the position of Wordsworth before Matthew Arnold made his famous selection. Beethoven, praised by all, is deeply loved by comparatively few, because his works have never yet in our minds been sorted and sifted as Matthew Arnold sifts those of the poet, explaining his object in a candid preface :

A mass of inferior work remains . . . embedding the first-rate work and clogging it, obstructing our approach to it, chilling, not unfrequently, the highwrought mood with which we leave it. To be recognized far and wide as a great poet, to be possible and receivable as a classic, Wordsworth needs to be relieved of a great deal of the poetical baggage which now encumbers him. To administer this relief is indispensable, unless he is to continue to be a poet for the few only, a poet valued far below his real worth by the world.

I am always pleased to see in the " Musical Times " the often-repeated suggestion of its editor that the best movements of Beethoven's symphonies should sometimes receive separate performance as independent concert items. I would not have the symphonies as wholes drop out of the repertory, any more than I would have the official shortened versions of Wagner's music dramas, which I have recently proposed, entirely supersede the full-length performances. But of the thirty-six symphony movements, some have much greater value than others, and I see little sense (in cyclic works of this period, where the movements have no organic connection) in the equal frequency of the performance of the inferior and superior movements. This, of course, applies equally to the string quartets.

To return to my main thesis—we ought to listen to every work of every composer, and every movement of every work, with as near a fresh mind as possible, honestly trying to apportion our admiration. And not only should we do this, but we should try also to judge fairly between one composer and another. To me Bach is greater than Handel, but I think it lamentable that our present Bach worship should carry with it the complete neglect of his great contemporary, as a few years ago the worship of Handel carried with it the neglect of Bach. And, agreeing that Mozart is, all things considered, perhaps a greater man than Haydn, I yet think this no excuse for our almost complete forgetfulness today of Haydn's symphonies, and our comparative neglect of his quartets. There is, I am glad to note, a growing popularity of the Elizabethans and of Purcell. It will, I fear, necessarily bring with it the neglect of the music of some other school. What, I wonder? The same unthinking public that swallows a composer whole, his bad parts and his good, rejects at the same time, equally unthinkingly and equally whole, some other composer of equal or almost equal merit, and opens its arms but slowly and reluctantly to any contemporary music which does not conform substantially to the methods of the past. There is no impediment to musical progress greater than the mind made up.

HANDEL AND BACH

I. Handel and the Horse's Leg

OUR bodies are nothing, says Samuel Butler; our work is everything. Shakespeare's real life never began till his body had been dead a hundred years, and "it is Handel's work, not the body with which he did the work, that pulls us half over London":

There is not an action of a muscle in a horse's leg upon a winter's night as it drags a carriage to the Albert Hall but is in connection with, and part outcome of, the force generated when Handel sat in his room at Gopsall and wrote the "Messiah." Think of all the forces which that force has controlled, and think, also, how small was the amount of molecular disturbance from which it proceeded. It is as though we saw a conflagration which a spark had kindled. This is the true Handel, who is a more living power among us one hundred and twenty-two years after his death than during the time he was amongst us in the body.

That was Butler's idea of survival after death. He wrote the words, evidently, in 1881, for Handel died in 1759. Since then that little bit of molecular disturbance at Gopsall has almost ceased to communicate itself to the legs of horses, but I see from the newspaper of the

day on which I write this that there are to be " special
services of express trains " to the Crystal Palace, and
that some people are expected to pay as much as three
guineas for a single seat to hear " Messiah " or " Judas
Maccabæus," or selections from " Israel in Egypt."
So the force is not yet spent.

Butler, of course, was a Handel enthusiast. Handel
interest, he says somewhere, pervaded his life " like
a ground bass " from the age of thirteen, when he first
heard some of the music. He drags Handel into pretty
nearly all his books. He and his friend Festing Jones
actually indulged in the sincerest form of flattery and
attempted composition in the Handelian style. I
have never yet been to the British Museum to ask for
" Narcissus," but the words of its final chorus used
to ring through my mind whenever I saw the advertisements of Treasury Loan and Housing Bonds.

> How blest the prudent man, the maiden pure,
> Whose income is both ample and secure,
> Arising from consolidated Three
> Per Cent. Annuities, paid quarterly.

The composers, we are told, remembered Handel's
treatment of the word " continually " in the Dettingen
Te Deum, where it is repeated fifty-one times (" if you
will say the word ' continually ' ten times on each of
your five fingers you will find it gives you an idea of
the fine effect produced ") and imitated it for their
words " paid quarterly." Public bodies issuing loans
might do worse than revive this chorus just now—
modernizing the reference to the amount of the divi-
dend, of course. It would be good propaganda if this

chorus could be issued as a National Loan Anthem.
Let Church help State !

I hardly think that there are many Handel enthusiasts of the Butler kind to-day. If there are I do
not come across them. Mr. Festing Jones must be
almost the last surviving member of a once numerous
body of people for whom Handel was everything, and
by whom Bach was hated as a crabbed old pedant.
Good old Rockstro, who taught Butler and Jones
counterpoint, was one of that sort. " He scolded
me once, and said he wondered how I could have
done such a thing as to call Handel ' one of the
greatest of all musicians,' referring to the great chords
in ' Erewhon.' I said that if he would look again
at the passage, he would find I had said, not that
Handel was ' one of the greatest,' but that he was ' the
greatest of all musicians,' on which he apologized."

But though these instructed enthusiasts perhaps no
longer exist, men who really knew music by other
composers, as Rockstro certainly did, and yet placed
Handel above them all, there are still lots of less
instructed ones. When I was a boy in a Yorkshire
town thirty years ago, the greatest music was oratorio ;
the greatest oratorios were " Messiah," " Elijah," and
" The Creation," the greatest of these (here we were,
of course, right) was " Messiah," and its greatest
pages those of the Hallelujah Chorus.

The real trouble with many of the surviving Handel
enthusiasts is not that they are too enthusiastic, but that
they are not enthusiastic enough. They have zeal, but
not according to knowledge. They worship an almost
unknown God. For whilst knowledge of Bach is ever

increasing, knowledge of Handel is ever diminishing. Less and less of him is heard. I was very glad to see that Mr. Nicholson performed " Israel in Egypt " at the Abbey the other day, and I see that at the Crystal Palace they are to give " selections " from this oratorio, and also " Judas Maccabæus." In my boyhood " Judas " (tout court) used to be almost as familiar a title as " Messiah," and I remember, as a small child, being curious to hear it and to see what sort of an oratorio could have been made out of the one personage of the New Testament I should have thought least susceptible of any such treatment. Now I think we have pretty well forgotten even " Judas," and " Jephthah " and " Joshua " and the rest have gone entirely. To-day I think Handel for most of us means (a) " Messiah," (b) the celebrated " Largo," and (c) The Dead March in " Saul." But I believe a few keener spirits still keep up " Angels ever bright and fair " and the (so-called) " Harmonious Blacksmith," and there is a hymn-tune Handel wrote for the Methodists (at the request of Mrs. Rich, wife of the theatre manager who afterwards dealt him such a blow by producing " The Beggar's Opera "), which people often sing to " Rejoice, the Lord is King," without knowing Handel wrote it.

Now why should this be ? It is as though Shakespeare were known only by " Hamlet " and a few flowery speeches from the other plays. If our Handelian friends really love Handel so much, why do they not perform more of him ? And why limit him to oratorio ? To mention but one branch of work, I never see his harpsichord works on the amateur's piano nowadays, and yet they contain lovely things. Here I differ from my friend, Dr. Ernest Walker, who condemns the " great bulk " as mere " jog-trot solid conventionalism of the kind that could apparently be reeled off *ad infinitum*, and virtually destitute of any invention worth the name." Handel in his keyboard pieces is not profound. He does not display the invention nor yet the depth of feeling we find in his contemporary Bach's wonderful three sets of Suites. But a lot of the stuff is delightful, and, from an amateur point of view, it has a great merit—you always get value for your practice. Handel was always " effective," and some of his pieces sound twice as difficult as they really are.

There is another complaint against Handelians, and a big one—their manner of performance of the choral works. Of this (a serious matter) I will say more anon. The main counts on the indictment are overgrown choirs and consequent lumbering style, and utter disregard of balance between the choral and orchestral forces. Still another complaint is the perpetuation of foolish legend. An example occurred in "The Times" the other day, where the sale was recorded of " Handel's Organ on which 'Messiah' was composed "! What sort of an idea, I wonder, has that Irish auctioneer of the process of composition? However, if his ingenious advertisement took a single jaunting-car along the road to Kilmore, a one-hundred-and-seventy-nine-year-old force is still moving horses' legs.

II.　Handel and Bach—As we Hear Them To-day

" Bach is a Gothic and Handel a Renaissance artist,"
said Arthur Johnstone, the brilliant critic of the
" Manchester Guardian." Some of my readers will
remember the saying, which appears on the very first
page of the volume of his collected criticisms published
by some loving friends of his when he died sixteen
years ago ; these will recall that he goes on to compare
the " St. Matthew Passion " and " Messiah " respect-
tively to Strasbourg Cathedral and St. Peter's at
Rome. Put this into terms of London architecture
and Bach is Westminster Abbey, Handel St. Paul's
Cathedral.

There is something in the idea. Bach's beauty is
at once more intimate and more mystical than Handel's.
His interlacing lines, each beautiful in itself, shape
themselves into beautiful patterns ; they enclose space,
as Handel's do, but this is not their first and most
apparent object. Bigness in Bach comes from within
him and seems often almost a by-product in his work.
Handel often uses lumps of masonry when Bach would
develop delicate decorative tracery or crossing ribs of
vaulting. Handel plans big mass and space effects ;
by means of size and contrast he strikes direct at our
feelings where Bach is intent simply on self-expression.

So I quite see what Johnstone means, but there is
another sense in which we might use architectural
analogy and class Bach and Handel together as Gothic,
and Haydn and Mozart as Renaissance. On a close
comparison of musical form, rather than spirit, this

is, indeed, the more correct analogy. Bach and Handel were (fundamentally) contrapuntal, and Haydn and Mozart (fundamentally) harmonic. The two former wove melodies together in their different voices, and chords resulted ; the two latter planned chord sequences and grew melodies and counterpoint out of these. Counterpoint was the very base in the one case and the ornament in the other, and that constitutes a very close analogy with Gothic architecture and Renaissance respectively.

All these analogies from one art to another are shifting, doubtful things, but it helps the understanding to make them. Personally, I think we place Handel most accurately when we compare him neither with St. Paul's nor with Westminster (as a whole), but rather with that now threatened west front of Westminster where Wren has imposed Renaissance ideas on a Gothic basis, or the west front of Milan Cathedral or some other piece of mingled expression in stone of the Gothic and Renaissance spirits. And in so far as purity of style is valued, we shall, I think, have to place Handel, however great, below Bach, just as we may place the west front at Westminster below the north transept, which, though also a restoration, is more consistent with itself and with the Abbey as a whole. From the point of practical performances, however, one thing is clear—we can conveniently consider the contemporaries, Bach and Handel, as representing one style, as presenting much the same problems to the conductor, and as exposing themselves to much the same dangers when they let their scores get into the hands of the modern choral-singer.

When a recent Bach Festival was held, I found that my brother critics went to it willingly. When the Handel Festival was announced, there was a rather general disposition to regard attendance as a disagreeable journalistic duty. There are some good reasons for the distinction, but, in a broad way, the faults and virtues of the one festival have been the faults and virtues of the other. In both cases the composer has been represented by a performance on a scale that he never in his life imagined as possible, and for which he did not provide, and in both cases there is, I think, the same justification—the pleasure of the performers themselves, rather than that of the audience.

This is something vital that is, I think, often overlooked. In the preparation of that Bach Festival, rather over three hundred and fifty keen musical people were given the pleasure of many weeks of rehearsal, week by week penetrating more deeply into the spiritual recesses of one of the greatest minds in history, labouring to reproduce in warm and well-shaped tone what he had been able to leave for them in the shape of mere cold notation. In the case of the Handel Festival, eight or ten times this number of performers enjoyed a similar experience. We are in danger sometimes of putting too high a value on perfection ; we would like every performance to be as technically polished as the cricket of two county teams ; but there is a place also for the village cricketers, and to have eleven hundred simple folk themselves handling bat and ball on their village greens is, in itself, a better thing than to have the same number watching twenty-two people doing the same thing with infinitely more skill. In some continental countries, if you want a choral performance you engage the opera chorus, or the choir of one of the churches. With us amateur choralism has become a tradition, and it is one worth keeping up. I commend to the superior person who sneers at these monster demonstrations the idea that they serve a most valuable social purpose. I shall not complain if it is charged against me that I sometimes put social values first and musical values second. At the Bach Festival I saw as plainly as anyone that the chorus carried " passengers," who were not working their way, not from any lack of will to do so, but because their powers had diminished with years. The singing was often magnificent, but it would have been more virile if a stern weeding-out had been decreed by the Committee before preparations had been allowed to begin. Yet if I were a committeeman I should have been reluctant to vote for it, and so I think would anyone who watched, as I did, the glowing faces of these three hundred and fifty inspired choralists. Exclude positively bad voices and really poor readers by all means, but do not be too exigent in the matter of either quality or volume of tone. The real justification of these big societies is arguably rather in the work they do at rehearsal than in the effect they produce at performance. There was one singer of eighty years of age in the Handel chorus. That gives him six more festivals before he registers a hundred. May he have them all before he joins Handel and the choral force on high !

The musical disadvantages of these huge performances are, I think, mainly two—(*a*) speed and brilliance in the degree the composers intended are almost impossible when the chorus is so unwieldy ; and (*b*) the inevitable disproportion between the choral and orchestral forces is distressing to anyone who knows the customs of the composers' own days and has studied their scores. Under both these heads I may say something further one of these days. Meantime I express my sympathy with a correspondent who has been a Handel Festival choralist for many years, and who represents, he says, a large number of his colleagues. He makes complaints as follows :

1. The announcements of this year's festival give the total of performers as 4,000, whereas, he tells me, the figure should be but 3,000. This, he thinks, led us all to feel disappointed when we heard the volume of tone. What do the authorities reply ? [1]

2. The soloists, he thinks, were (with some exceptions) inadequate, and he makes a modest suggestion that " it would be well for music of this description if the world could produce singers like Trebelli, Grisi, Titiens, Albani, Patey, and Patti."

The critics, he thinks, are to blame for the " inferiority " of the present soloists : " If they slanged them with comparisons to the great prima donnas of past years, surely something would be done to improve things and find Pattis, Pateys, Sims Reeves and Marios, etc." This sounds easy enough. I must try it !

---

[1] They replied nothing, but three years later, in 1923, made exactly the same announcement. Again the names of singers and players, as given in full in their programmes, amounted to one thousand less than the total announced.

3. Though the choir "kept up marvellous tone without signs of exhaustion," they had to do it "with such poor refreshments as the male choir buffet provided—ham rolls at 3*d*. and pork pies 1*s*." Here I think our friend has our sympathy, and I give him mine, the more readily since I myself was particularly well supplied with bodily sustenance, the Handel Festival being the only event I attend at which courteous gentlemen in frock-coats seek out the critics and offer them free tickets for lunch and tea. Putting two and two together, I wonder if it is not really the fault of those frock-coated gentlemen that we do not now get the " Pattis, Pateys, Sims Reeves and Marios." (Mem. To inquire—Were the critics fed in the old days ?).

SHAKESPEARE'S MUSIC: A THEORY

IT is curious that in the mass of critical discussions of Shakespeare that is always appearing, one subject is overlooked. It always has been overlooked. You will find no mention of it in the eighteenth and nineteenth-century Shakespeare commentary and criticism collected in the great Furness " Variorum " edition, or in anything written since. It is a question of Shakespeare's so frequent use of music, but it is not referred to in the two or three books upon the music of Shakespeare.

In all these works Shakespeare's music is treated of as " incidental," to use the actor-manager's phrase in his advertisements—a phrase by which the actor-manager misleads himself, often with most unfortunate results for Shakespeare. My contention is that the large amount of music for which Shakespeare calls is, most of it, not " incidental " but vital—a part of his very dramatic scheme, an element upon which he relies to help him out at moments when speech and action are insufficient.

The proper way to approach this subject is to examine the places where Shakespeare calls for music. A certain number of these we can put aside at once as examples of true " incidental " use. Music is here a trimming on the edge of drama, not a part of its stuff.

194

Such, for instance, is the masque music in " As You Like It," which the dramatist dragged in because he thought his public would like a little musical diversion at this point ; the ball music in " Romeo and Juliet," which came in just because you could not have a ball without music ; the banquet music in " Antony and Cleopatra " and " Coriolanus," Falstaff's tavern music, Cassio's music outside Othello's lodging, Glendower's minstrel music in " Henry IV," the merry-making music in " The Winter's Tale "—and so forth. But it is a different thing when we come to look at many other instances of the use of music, and my own conviction is that if these be carefully studied there will be found lying behind them evidence of a great purpose. You will find case after case where Shakespeare used music in order to produce the emotions of the " supernatural." (I have put that word into inverted commas because I want to use it in a rather special way, a wider way than is, perhaps, common ; this will be seen in a moment.)

Anyone who will take the trouble to copy out and compare the hundreds of musical allusions and passages, involving the use of music in Shakespeare will, I think, find that they are frequently (perhaps generally) associated with activity on a special plane. Music with Shakespeare is possessed of magical properties. His fairies have music ; his witches have music ; sometimes his ghosts have music. Music and madness go together, music and love, music and healing, music and death. It may at first seem fanciful to class all these things together as " supernatural," but reflection will show, I think, that as a convenient term the word is justified.

When these things are toward, the dramatist has to take us out of our everyday selves ; we are to be made to feel ourselves in the presence of the magic of witchcraft or the magic of love (which is surely no less a magic), to feel the magical awe of a return from the grave, or the awe of the departure of a soul (which is no less an awe), to see minds disordered brought to order again and bodies apparently dead brought to life (and this is magical too). If Shakespearean students will take the trouble to look into his practice in the use of music, I think they will be surprised to find how often the passages in which he calls for it fall into one or other of these various categories and a few others like them.

In all this we see, I think, the practical hand of a playwright who knew his job. He had a stage that projected into the pit and into the open air ; there was no means of darkening it or of using coloured light, such as the modern stage depends on at moments like those I have described. He had no scenery— or none to speak of. He could make little appeal through the eye in these " supernatural " moments, so he made his appeal through the ear. Moreover, as Sir Hubert Parry once pointed out when I discussed the subject in his presence, Shakespeare had in his theatre an audience to whom that appeal through the ear might be safely made. England in those days was intensely musical ; music was then loved and practised amongst all classes. I do not admit that we are nowadays (as is so often charged against us) an unmusical people, but I think nobody can deny that the emotions of the average Elizabethan were more susceptible to the musical appeal than those of the average theatre-goer to-day.

Let us take a practical example of the difficulty of the dramatist. The great quarrel between Brutus and Cassius is just over. The friends are reconciled and have parted for the night. The excitement of the audience has been worked up by the quarrel. The atmosphere is not that which the dramatist feels is needed for the appearance of Cæsar's ghost, with its thrilling warning. This is just the place where the modern dramatist would rely upon a preliminary turning down of the lights and the appearance of the ghost in almost complete darkness, draped in white, with bright limelight playing on him alone—or some such device. Shakespeare could not do that : the whole thing was to be done in the light of day, and his chief reliance is on music. Brutus calls on his boy attendant :

BRUTUS : Canst thou hold up thy heavy eyes awhile
And touch thy instrument a strain or two ?
LUCIUS : Ay, my lord, an't please you.
BRUTUS : It does, my boy :
I trouble thee too much, but thou art willing.
(*Music and a Song.*)

All is now still ; the two soldiers present in the tent sleep, the boy also. Only Brutus wakes, and he takes up a book, finds the page turned down where he last left off reading, sits, and is quietly settling to read when—the ghost of Cæsar enters.

It will be noticed here how cleverly Shakespeare

calms down his audience—prepares their mood, and
very subtly awakens a feeling of expectation of something awesome to come. This is the equivalent of
many a passage in Beethoven, where a striking theme
is preceded by a passage of significance chiefly as a
preparation of the mind of the audience for what is
to follow. Many such passages must have been after-
thoughts of the composer : he has quite evidently
written, or thought out, the theme he means to introduce at that particular part of his work, and has then
set to work to produce a passage that shall prepare
the mood of his audience. It sounds unstudied, even
spontaneous, but was probably the result of much
thought and experiment. The passage which precedes the recapitulation in the first movement of the
" Eroica " Symphony is a familiar example.

Let us consider a few more cases. If you will look
through your " Midsummer Night's Dream," and
imagine all the fairy passages performed without
their music, you will realize the loss we should have
suffered if Shakespeare had not observed the tradition
that the little people are musicians. But to the Elizabethan theatre-goer, under the open-air conditions
already alluded to, the loss would have been much
greater. Our modern stage-manager gets at us through
our eyes where his sixteenth-century predecessor would
have got at us through our ears. " You spotted snakes "
and its chorus, " Philomel, with melody," are not mere
embellishments, but part of the play, and though the
calling for music to effect the spell of sleep (so that
Bottom's ass's head may be removed) is, looked at from
one point of view, a survival of the old association of

music and magic, from another it is a stage-manager's device for making credible a bit of supernatural interference with the affairs of men.

So, too, with the witches. Of course, here, again, music was traditionally associated with the supernatural. When we read in " News from Scotland " (1591) of one of King James's witch trials, we find plenty of music in the evidence :

" Agnes Sampson being brought before the King's Majesty and his council, confessed that upon the night of All-Halloweven last, shee was accompanied as well with the persons aforesaid, as also with a great many other witches, to the number of two hundreth ; and that all they together went to sea, each one in a riddle or cive, and went into the same very substantially, with flaggons of wine, making merrie, and drinking by the way, in the same riddles or cives to the kirke of North Barrick in Lowthian ; and that after they had landed took handes on the lande, and daunced this reill or short daunce, singing :

> Commer goe ye before, commer goe ye,
> Gif ye will not goe before, commer let me.

At which time, she confessed that this Geillis Duncan (a servant girl) did goe before them, playing this reill or daunce upon a small trumpe, called a Jewes trump, until they entered the kirk of North Barrick. These confessions made the King in a wonderful admiration, and sent for the saide Geillis Duncan, who upon the like trump did play the saide daunce before the Kinges Maiestie ; who in respect of the strangenes of these matters, tooke great delight to be present at their examinations."

And when Shakespeare in " Macbeth " showed us the witches at their work, of course he had to give them their customary music. But he had another object than merely to observe custom, I think. Hecate, the Queen of the Witches, is called to mysterious music heard behind the scenes, coming apparently from nowhere ; the witches dance round the cauldron to music. The cauldron sinks to the coarse, rough tone of the Elizabethan hautboys. Then appears the greatest of the apparitions Macbeth is to see—the " Show of eight kings " and the ghost of Banquo, and (both to keep up the realism and sustain the emotion of the audience) the witches profess to " cheer " Macbeth with a dance to some more unearthly and invisibly made music, after which they vanish. It is said that Shakespeare wrote his Scottish play of " Macbeth " to please James I—who as James VI of Scotland had made those curious investigations into witchcraft. I think he put his witches in with a business purpose, and to carry off all the difficulties of enacting deeds of darkness on, say, a bright May afternoon on the Bankside, he added plenty of creepy music, no doubt specially composed for him by one of the many fine composers living in London—some of them then of European fame.

There are a good many miraculous cures in Shakespeare—lame things they would be but for the music that accompanies them. Cerimon, in " Pericles," has the body of Thaisa, found in the sea, brought before him. He gives hasty orders for a fire to be made and for clothes and appliances to be brought, and then adds :

" The rough and woful music that we have,
   Cause it to sound, beseech you.
The viol once more : how thou stirr'st, thou block !
The music there ! I pray you give her air.
Gentleman,
This queen will live : nature awakes ; a warmth
Breathes out of her ; she hath not been entranced
Above five hours : see how she 'gins to blow
Into Life's flower again ! "

Dramatically that must have been most effective. Drugs would have been prosaic and unconvincing, for they would only have operated on Thaisa, whereas music operated at the same time on the minds of the audience. Later in the same play, Pericles himself is cured—after a long period of speechless misery—by music. Similarly, of course, King Lear is cured of his madness by " soft music playing," by the doctor's orders. Compare with this the earlier case of King Saul.

Music and love are associated with Shakespeare, and again we see the " supernatural " use of music, for who that is in love would admit that he is walking on the everyday plane ? A very long essay would be needed to expound Shakespeare's use of music here, and a short, but very interesting one might be written about his use of music to awe his audience on the approach or occurrence of death. As for " The Tempest," that is a play that is full of the supernatural—and of music. All this, duly pondered upon, will be found to constitute an appeal to the thoughtful actor-manager. Where is he ?

WORDS AND MUSIC

I. "WE WANT THE WORDS"

ONE Monday morning lately I received this
letter from a reader :

I have been to the Albert Hall concert this afternoon, where an accomplished artist, good to look
on, and with good platform manners, sang good songs,
and sang them well—but for one thing. That one
thing was so irritating that I have felt compelled to
sit down and write to you in the hope that you can
handle it in the "Observer" soon. It is the interpolation of aspirates in the middle of words sung to more
than one note. One song, for instance, was "The Lass
with the Delicate Air." This was practically spoilt
by it. The conclusion became : " *How to wi-hin the-
he de-hear la-hass wi-hith the-he de-he-he-he-li-hi-ca-hate
air.*" I have noticed that nearly every professional
singer does this sort of thing, particularly in opera,
and no doubt it helps a lot, and is a trick of the trade
in long florid passages. But there can be no possible
need to use the trick in a simple and delicate song
like this.

Cruelty comes naturally to a critic, and mercilessly
I round upon this plaintiff and make him the defendant
in a counter-action. It is he and the like of him who

have made the singers what they are, for, speaking generally, it is the complaisance of audiences that has brought about the degradation of speech in song, as it has brought about many other vocal evils. Note that this gentleman, whilst very properly irritated at a singer's mannerism in the concert-hall, would (for so I read him) in the theatre have been somewhat tolerant of the same defect. So long as singers get their applause, whatever articulatory atrocities they commit, so long will the English language as heard from the mouths of singers remain a disgusting and often incoherent jumble. A good deal has been said of the heroism of the bold individual who protested against vocal encores and encored encores and re-encored encores on the recent Albert Hall Beecham-Butt festival occasion. " We want to hear the orchestra ! " he cried. Who will now, in the same place, cry, " We want to hear the words " ?

My view that the public are at least as much to blame for the bad articulation of singers as the singers themselves is confirmed by a singer :

The Anglo-Saxon race is the most good-natured in the world. It has a peculiar horror of wounding the feelings of the public performer, and out of sheer good-fellowship it puts its telescope to its blind eye rather than hurt. This happy relationship between performer and audience has made public singing a pleasant life for the professional wherever the English language is spoken. But, like every other form of *laisser aller*, it has worked for harm unconsciously. The " *Basta ! basta !* " of the Italians may be cruel in its immediate application, but it is cruel to be kind. It is a protest against the lowering of certain standards long accepted by the people as compulsory. The singer who has not trained himself to them knows what to expect. He makes no complaint, and generally tries to right himself, for he has had the inestimable benefit of directly realizing where and why he falls short. The British singer has suffered badly from the other extreme. For his faults of diction he is hardly to blame, seeing that his public has never remotely demanded a standard of him. That public has either never realized that it has a language of incomparable beauty of its own, or has from long acquiescence in bad habits learned to accept those bad habits as inevitably associated with the musical expression of words.

That comes, of course, from the pithiest book upon singing ever written, Plunket Greene's " Interpretation in Song." The author gives some bad examples of English as she is sung. Other writers on the subject have done this too, but, so far as I recall, this is the only one of them who has differentiated between the various voices—the contralto, " by far the worst offender . . . who has only one object, to make her voice sound. . . . Her proximity to the note on which she expects to make her most brilliant fog-horn effect can be gauged by the brightening of her eye " ; the cathedral-bass with his broad " Au-maim " for " Amen," and " hawly " for " holy " ; the tenor and soprano who " sin more by omission than commission," and so forth. Here is a contralto example (from Barnby's " When the flowing tide came in ") :

" Mawther-a," he cry-eed-a, "gaw wortch-a tha
    ty-eed-a,
Arz it cawmeth-a arp-a too Lynn-a.
For-a fou-url-a or fayr-a oi weel-a be they-ra
When-a tha flaw-inga ty-eed-a cawms in-a."

Santley (" The Art of Singing ") quotes from a
performance of " Judas Maccabæus " :

      " Olletteturnullhonnurs crownnhis na-em,"
And, from the same oratorio :
                    " Sounddannalaam."

Ffrangcon-Davies (" The Singing of the Future ")
combating the idea that tone production is a justification, insists that " the quickest way to fine tone
is *viâ* fine pronunciation," but abstains from actual
quotation. Dr. Coward (" Choral Technique and
Interpretation ") complains of " Moighty in bottle,"
of " His morcy " (in " Elijah "), of the neglect of
consonants, producing " Hell, Lor ! " instead of
" Help, Lord," and, on the other hand, of the over-
anxiety about consonants, leading to such excesses as
" Helpa, Lorda." He also warns against the over-
doing of the dangerous " s," and in this connection
I would say that, for my part, I have never yet heard
a performance of " The Hymn of Jesus " where the
spoken counterpoint, as we may call it, upon page 6
of the vocal score, produced any other effect than :

     " Glory to the Holy Ssspit, Ssspit, Ssspit,"
and so on to the eighth hissing repetition as the
various voices read the word. Holst, however, in
my judgment, has been indiscreet here in the problem
in choral unanimity he has set his conductors.

For, of course, it is sometimes the composers who are to blame. Blanche Marchesi (" Singer's Pilgrimage ") admits that in " The Dusk of the Gods," on the high A flat, " Siegfried, selig grüsst dich dein Weib," she always sang " Sagfrod," and defends herself by the argument, " If I really sang ' Siegfried,' and pushed out an ' e ' on the top note, I should soon have no voice left at all "—which is probable enough ; moreover, as even purist-Plunket admits, " the pure ' ee ' on a soprano top A would sound like a slate-pencil." If the composer asks for impossibilities or risky improbabilities, he can't have them, and that's all about it, but, short of these, English or any other language should be sung as it is spoken. Or, rather (and this is important), it should be sung as it ought to be spoken. For the fact is, that in everyday speech there are lots of words we should miss entirely but for the context, and the proof of that is that when we get a word which is unassisted by its context, as is the case with a personal name in an introduction, we almost invariably lose it altogether.

II. " A Concerto on the Larynx "

If you want to make a nail do its business, you must violently and repeatedly knock it on the head. The same is true of singers, so I make no apology for pursuing the subject of one of their most amazing failures—the failure to convey to us the literary sense (if any) of their songs. Some of these people may perhaps by now have noticed that when, by some extraordinary exertion, they do get their words over to us, the surprise and delight of one particular member of their audience are likely to be communicated to a larger public, and that when they do not do so his irritation is equally likely to be publicly expressed. The fact is, that we critics have for a long time been too easy with the spoiled darlings of the musical profession, and that, from our neglect, they have come to take as their professional motto, *Vox et præterea nihil.*

The evil, though it seems to us especially " rampant " just now, is, I suppose, as old as the hills. The other day I chanced to drop into a second-hand bookseller's and with my first glance to make acquaintance with a book upon the subject, of which I had long known, but which I had never before seen—the " Observations on Vocal Music " of William Kitchener, M.D., published in 1821. The advertisements at the back and front of this book remind me that the author wrote also " Practical Observations on Telescopes, Opera Glasses, and Spectacles," and I think I am right in saying that he was the writer of " The Cook's Oracle " (he gives in my book, by the way, a recipe for beef-tea) and of " The Art of Invigorating and Prolonging Life " (I am sure plainer speech on the part of singers would prolong mine, but perhaps this is not an object with them), and was also editor of a collection of " English Melodies," of which he claimed to possess " two hundred and fifty folio volumes, comprising every English opera which has been printed from the commencement of that kind of Drama till 1810." Altogether, a very versatile medical musical adviser. Let us give him attention !

"The warbling of sounds without the distinct articulation of the words," says Kitchener, "does not deserve to be called Singing ; it is merely playing upon the Voice—a Concerto upon the Larynx." (That, I think, is a happy phrase, worthy of a music-loving physiologist.) "Few ears are more susceptible of the charms of Music than my own—however, I still consider it but as the Varnish, and Poetry the Picture—some Musicians have treated them so differently, one would suppose they considered the Words as merely blank canvas for them to display the varnish upon." If this metaphor is to be accepted, then I suppose my invitations to first-nights must be considered courteous invitations to be present on Varnishing Day, and I would like to take this opportunity of asking whether in the large audience that heard the first London performance of "Fête Galante" there was one person who heard one word of the quartet with which the composer has accompanied the dumb-motion Pierrot play, with the very object that it should explain to us, action by action, what the players are doing. I casually asked a lady present whether she had caught any of the words, and she replied with surprise, "Are there any ? I thought it was just written as a piece of vocalization !" In other words, "A Concerto for Four Larynxes"!

Kitchener goes on to tell of his friendship with Mme. Mara, and of a conversation with her in which, after he had pressed her to bring out an edition of the Handel songs, in which she excelled, "with the embellishments, etc., with which she enriched them," "this inimitable Singer replied, 'Indeed, my good

friend, you attribute my success to a very different
source than the real one—it was not what I did, but
the manner in which I did it ; I am sure it was to
my expression of the Words that I owe everything ;
people have often said to me, Madame Mara, why
do you not introduce more pretty things—and passages
—and graces into your songs ?   I said, these pretty
things, etc., are very pretty to some, but the proper
expression of the Words and the Music is a great
deal better.' "   He goes on to tell that " whenever
Mara was encored in a Song, on her return home she
seldom retired to rest without first inventing a new
Cadence for the next performance of it.   Here is an
example for the young Singers ! ! ! "   So it is to be
sure, and worthy of any number of the doctor's lavish
notes of exclamation !   We don't nowadays want
young singers to " invent cadences," nor are we
fond of " enrichments," or " pretty things and passages
and graces," but the idea of paying an audience for an
encore by a little extra practice against the next performance is a good one, and may perhaps be novel
to some of my singer readers.   I suggest that they
should carry it out by going home and intoning the
multiplication table, or " Thirty days have Septem-
ber," or " Eena-meena-myna-mo," or the terms of
their contract for their next tour, or any other piece
of poetical literature, in such a way that they feel
sure that any intelligent native of Bechuanaland,
seated one Queen's Hall or Covent Garden length
distant (we will say nothing about the Albert Hall),
could safely take it as a lesson in pure English.
" Polly," Kitchener tells us, was one of Mara's great

successes : despite the fact that she did not " speak English natively," she made a great effect through her expression of the words. It is some time since I heard our charming present-day " Polly," but when I did, much as I found to admire in her singing and acting, her words almost constantly eluded me, as did those of several of her otherwise capable companions. Since then some " Polly " gramophone records have been issued, but, so far as the poems go, I can make little of them. Of course, our singing teaching is at present often very defective in this matter, as Kitchener complains it was in his day. Too many teachers seem to be content with the description " Voice Producer," so much so, that the description " Word Producer " on a brass plate would probably cause a sensation.

A good many health hints for vocalists are given, as we should expect from the profession of our author. I have not space here to repeat these at any length, but it seems a duty to pass on the advice to shun gargles. And to " tune the throat to a pitch of healthy vibration," there is nothing better than " one of the strong Peppermint Lozenges made by Smith, Fell Street, Wood Street." No doubt this Smith has a successor. At all events, both Smiths and Peppermint Lozenges are common enough, and if the members of our opera companies will undertake to sing in future in such a way that we shall all know what they are singing about, I am sure there are plenty of us who, in grateful admiration, will gladly linger about the stage door with boxes of lozenges.

CHORAL SOCIETY PROBLEMS

I SUPPOSE everybody admits that choral singing is one of the most characteristic of our national musical activities, and is agreed that it is one in which it would be very regrettable to find any decline. Some of the special difficulties with which it is at present faced are, therefore, a fit subject for our attention. I take up the subject at the instigation of a reader who is conductor of a choral society in the Midlands, and who writes as follows :

Would you consider the possibility of dealing with the difficulties of the smaller choral societies ? We need advice, and a little sympathy would encourage us to go forward or correct our precocious aspirations.
Take my own case. We lose on every concert—that goes without saying—but we don't worry about that. We want to do bigger works ; the *big* works. My chorus consists of about 100, and we could *sing* "Gerontius." But (1) our hall isn't big enough to accommodate an adequate orchestra, especially all the brass, and we couldn't possibly get them all on the stage ; (2) we certainly couldn't afford them ; and (3) if we could, they would swamp the chorus. Now my question arises—are we justified in attempting works of such dimensions just because the conductor and chorus are capable of doing their part ?

I enclose one of our programmes, so that you may see the orchestra we usually engage [a dozen strings, two each of flutes, oboes, clarinets, bassoons, horns, and trumpets, one trombone, timpani, and piano as harp]. Even now they are packed like herrings, with the strings sitting in all manner of positions to obtain bowing space, and the vocal soloists among the instrumentalists. When we do an oratorio I have to spend considerable time rescoring the parts, where missing instruments have had solo or essential parts.

Must we abandon our ambition of doing " big " works because we can't get the orchestra, or may we use a smaller orchestra and fill in on the piano or harmonium ? Do you think our greatest composers realize that they prevent dozens of capable societies performing their works by the huge band they require ?

I know that the writer of this letter has colleagues all over the country who might have written to me in almost the same words. Largely the difficulties that have arisen are those of money ; concerts now cost more to carry through, and the halls, in many cases, will no longer hold a paying audience. Thus the music critic of the " Yorkshire Post," Mr. Herbert Thompson, expressed himself the other day to the following effect :

The programme of last evening's concert of the York Musical Society, at which " The Dream of Gerontius " was performed, was prefaced by a note apologizing for the shortcomings of the concert-hall, and indeed it is a misfortune that the city should be without a room suitable for performances on a large scale, spacious enough to hold a paying audience (it was calculated that, with every seat taken, a loss of £50 would necessarily be incurred), and convenient enough to seat it without discomfort.

I have been in correspondence with the conductor of the society mentioned, Dr. E. C. Bairstow, organist of York Minster, and conductor also of the Leeds Philharmonic Society and the Bradford Festival Choral Society. His view is that the solution of his difficulties and those of the first writer would lie in the provision of more choral works scored for small orchestra :

You can see from the " Yorkshire Post " paragraph how we are fixed. We have to give one concert without orchestra to help to pay for another with orchestra, and supplement this with " patrons " who subscribe money without receiving any *quid pro quo*. No doubt works with small orchestra would be a god-send, if we could find sufficient to go round, and I must quote Holst's " Hymn of Jesus " as an example of what can be done in this way. Perhaps you know that, by means of small notes in the score and cues in the wind parts, it is possible to perform this work without trombones and with only two horns and ordinary wood-wind. Vaughan Williams has also done a similar thing to a smaller extent with his " Sea Symphony," and there are many works now scored for a very large orchestra which might receive the same treatment and yet remain very effective.

A totally different solution is proposed by Mr. Hugh S. Roberton, conductor of the Glasgow Orpheus Choir, a remarkable body, of great fame in the North, which has several times given performances in our

Royal Albert Hall and Queen's Hall, and has travelled extensively in its concert-giving.

Your correspondent raises an interesting point. Firstly, how many works are there that are worth doing at all—three or four of Bach's, one or two of Handel's, " Gerontius," " Hiawatha," and one or two others ? All this talk of " works " is in need of straightening out. We do not worship bulk in pictorial art, nor in sculpture, nor in literature. The worship of bulk is a Victorian legacy. But surely the day of long sermons and long poems ("Night Thoughts," " The Task," etc.) is over. And would choral societies not do better to turn some of their attention to the rich store of unaccompanied music, leaving the performance of " works " for an odd festival occasion ? They would then improve their technique, and their tone, and their intelligence, and their self-reliance, and make themselves more fit to do " Gerontius " and the " B Minor," etc., when the time came.

The average choral society doing " works " is lamentably weak musically. In nine cases out of ten the band pulls them through. Why blunder along like this when the way of choral salvation lies through the unaccompanied song and madrigal ? Indeed, the position is this—many choral societies have ceased to do serious music, and have gone at a bound from " Messiah " to " The Country Girl," because (1) " works " did not pay, (2) the musical outlook of the singers and conductor was so meagre that they could not see any other way out.

In Scotland, when the big choral bodies held sway, " doing " the " Messiah," etc., musical life was stagnant. It was when small bodies formed themselves to do really artistic work that we started to move. I consider that a small choir singing, say, " My love dwelt " of Elgar's, to the height of its artistic capacity, does more to advance musical art than 10,000 singers hugger-muggering through a so-called " work." And when we get a network of these small expert and artistic bodies, then will come the time to join them up, and really *do* the " B Minor," etc.

Commenting on the suggestion of Dr. Bairstow that composers should be more considerate in their orchestral demands, another correspondent reminds me that not only Holst's " Hymn of Jesus," but also his " Ode to Death," is arranged in such a way that either larger or smaller orchestra may be used. This same correspondent, Mr. Harold Brooke, conductor of the Novello Choir, says : " What about the Bach Cantatas, with their small orchestras ? " But adds : " Maybe the fact that they usually include for the choir only one chorus and a chorale is against their finding favour with choral societies." I do not think this circumstance should be so frequently a barrier to the performance of these works as it seems to be. At all events, on occasions when a programme calling for a small orchestra has been decided upon, a Bach Cantata might often suitably take its place as a part of it.

This writer then goes on to allude to the suggestion of Mr. Roberton, that " the way of choral salvation lies through the unaccompanied part-song and madrigal." He states : " The Novello Choir has come to exactly the type of programme advocated ; for about three years now we have been working on those

lines and with never a regret for the abandoned ' big '
things." I note, however, that this choir has not
adopted what we may call the full Glasgow policy,
inasmuch as at its recent concert in the Bishopsgate
Institute it performed not only a group of madrigals
by Wilbye, but also Purcell's " King Arthur," Holst's
" St. Paul's Suite for Strings," etc. I should say
that by devoting some concerts to purely unaccompanied works and others largely to works with or
for small orchestra, it has struck the happy mean.
Another conductor, Mr. Bernard Haines, an amateur
musician and conductor of the choral society at
Faringdon, Berkshire, a body of sixty-five voices,
confirms the success of the policy of adopting a
mixture of unaccompanied choral works and choral
works requiring but a small orchestra :

It is one of the most difficult problems (having
regard to the size of our chorus, and the present high
cost of publishing music) to select works suitable for
performance at our annual concert. The size of the
hall and stage will only allow a small orchestra of
strings, flute and piano (a dozen performers). It
has been our aim during the last three years to take
what you describe as " choral music in the lesser
forms." . . . We supplement our programme with
vocal and instrumental solos. . . . Fortunately the
financial results have steadily improved at each
concert, and have resulted in a balance in hand at
the last two concerts—not bad, I think, considering
that we have to call in professional aid for the vocal
solos, viola, double-bass, and flute.

A practical suggestion towards the reduction of

the financial problem in connection with the smaller choral societies is made by another writer, Mr. Cyril Winn, conductor, I believe, of a London suburban society :

If I had no such " locus " for my own choral society, I should boldly approach ministers of the various churches in the neighbourhood, arouse their interest, get permission for a performance, and then rehearse some " non-secular " work for performance in church. As there seems to be a scarcity of purely secular works, my suggestion is not so unreasonable as it might otherwise appear. That is what I am going to do next year—with a collection at the doors. Having an organ at my disposal, I can dispense with brass and wood-wind.

My only fear about this plan is that the absurd denominational prejudices of this country may affect the size of the audience. In an open-minded country like America the idea might work, but here I have doubts. Still, the plan should certainly be tried.

A question not yet touched upon is this : Is there a decline in public support for choral music ? I have a rather sad letter from the secretary of a large and long-established suburban society, Mr. Harry B. Longhurst, of the Dulwich Philharmonic Society, which gives fine programmes in the Crystal Palace. He agrees that smaller choirs should do smaller works, but continues : " Our society is perfectly able to produce practically any work written, as we have to-day a fully trained choir of about 180 voices and an amateur orchestra of forty-five, which only needs the usual additions of wood-wind and brass at concerts.'' But, he continues :

   To produce a programme such as we present, over £100 is necessarily expended, yet the sale of tickets at the box office and through agents during the past season has averaged but £12 per concert, or the equivalent of 192 seats at 1s. 3d. each. . . . If it were not for the members themselves and their immediate friends, amongst whom they can dispose of tickets, it would be impossible to carry on. I look in vain for a remedy.

Our Glasgow mentor would, of course, suggest an heroic remedy in such a case. Personally, I should be sorry to see the abandonment of big works by such a society, but, in favour of the Glasgow view, I must in honesty point out that eighteen tenors and twenty-seven basses (where *are* the men nowadays ? I fear these proportions are but too typical) offer a very poor balance to seventy sopranos and forty-eight contraltos. The bold policy would be, I suppose, to scale down the crew all round to something near the dimensions of its smallest factor (necessarily securing by rigid selection a heightened efficiency), and then with a smaller ship to sail out into the wide seas of unaccompanied choralism. Whether, if I were a member of the committee, I should dare to propose this is another question. Choral societies do not exist solely for the concert performances, and to rob about eighty keen choralists of their weekly practice-pleasure is a proposal that needs a little consideration. Besides, I do not know the Dulwich ladies !

   This question of balance of vocal parts is another

thorny one. A good many conductors, secretaries, and others have lately very kindly sent me actual figures. Dr. Henry Coward gives me the figures of two of his famous choirs as follows : Leeds Choral Union, 120—95—67—95 ; Huddersfield Choral Society, 117—92—64—60. Mr. J. H. Green, for very many years honorary secretary of the Leeds Philharmonic Society, rightly distinguishes between choruses selected for important festival purposes, to a previously agreed scheme of balance, and societies dependent upon local and varying conditions. As an example of the selected choir, he gives me these figures of the " Leeds Chorus " which, under Stanford's conductor-ship, went to sing in Paris in 1906, a body which, I can personally testify, provided a magnificent ensemble, and which, as I well remember, evoked the most flattering remarks from French musicians in the audience. The original scheme, Mr. Green tells me, was 60—50—40—50 (picked from 700 applicants from all over Yorkshire), but, later, some few additions were made, chiefly to the soprano and contralto sections, with a few basses. For twenty-one years Mr. Green was largely responsible for the balance of his society ; he discussed it frequently with visiting conductors, such as Barnby, Richter, Henschel, Stanford, Wood, Walford Davies, and others, and his own opinion that on the occasion of this Paris visit the ideal was attained must be accepted as of value.

Dr. W. G. Whittaker, founder and conductor of the Newcastle-on-Tyne Bach Choir, has deliberately kept his figures low, believing, I think, that for flexibility in Bach performance you need a small but efficient body. He gives his parts as 11—10—10—10, i.e. equality, but for an extra soprano included, lest, in case of illness, his lower parts might become heavier than his higher. In the eight-part work of the B minor Mass he simply divides ; in the five-part choruses he adds ten extra sopranos, a very obvious and frequent cause of failure to balance being thus abolished ; in the six-part Sanctus he further adds ten contraltos. I must admit that to me his scheme looks perfect. But not every conductor, of course, could find able and willing extra singers ; this is how we shall sing Bach in heaven. A body of high standing in the Midlands is the William Woolley Choral Society of Nottingham. Mr. Woolley's figures are surprisingly different from Dr. Whittaker's, since with the same number of tenors, (i.e. ten) he associates eighteen sopranos, eighteen contraltos, and thirteen basses. As this conductor remarks, quality and quantity of tone count more than number of voices, which, as will be noted in Nottingham, is an implied compliment for his men ! Mr. Harry Cooper, who is, I think, connected with the famous Blackpool Competition Festival, tells me that choirs of sixty heard at this festival are divided almost invariably as follows : 16—16—14—16.

Here I leave the question of balance, merely expressing the opinion that the disparities shown above are, on the whole, rather too great to be explained entirely on the grounds of local variation of voice-values, and that the subject seems, therefore, to call for a rather closer consideration. To this I wish to add an opinion on re-testing. I am, in London, constantly hearing choirs many of the members of which, though they retain their splendid enthusiasm, have obviously lost a large part of their vocal force and quality. The only efficient and tactful means of avoiding this seems to me to be the one adopted by the Glasgow Orpheus Choir—annual re-examination of *every singer* by a panel of independent musicians associated with the conductor. If this plan were more generally adopted, the standard of British choral singing would in five years rise 25 per cent.

High cost of printed music is an important point raised by several conductors. It will be remembered that Mr. Harold Brooke, of the Novello Choir, recommended Bach cantatas as being performable with small and inexpensive orchestra. Dr. Whittaker has performed over sixty of these, but says that one-and-eightpence or so for works containing often but two choral numbers (the rest being solos) is more than the average society can afford. He pleads for separate issue of the choruses of these works, and also of such things as Purcell's " Dido," " King Arthur," and " Fairy Queen." Mr. Frederick Ely, of the Ayr Burgh Choir, supports the use of unaccompanied works, but adds: " Madrigals, if overdone, somehow pall a little, I think, on account of the want of human interest in the words. The ' silly shepherds ' with their eternal ' fa-las,' and the ' fair Oriana,' get on one's nerves after a time." He adds: " What composers should do is to copy Elgar in his ' Black Knight,' possibly the best of his shorter works, scored for single ' winds,' and therefore not too expensive, and also economical of platform space." Mr. George W.

Chalk, who is connected, I think, with the Glasgow Choral Union (a body with the advantage of association with the Scottish Orchestra), thinks there are more works available for less favoured societies that can only afford and accommodate a small orchestra than is generally realized ; he approves, of course, of the cultivation of unaccompanied music, but would not have societies too readily assent to the view that performance of " works " is to be decried. In this connection, Mr. W. Murphy, a London reader, quotes Poe—" Grandeur in any of its moods first startles, then excites, then fatigues—depresses," but thinks that the practice of including in a programme one or two choruses from the great " works " might be more general. Mr. J. W. Waterer, hon. sec. of the South London Philharmonic Society, recounts the success that has followed the policy of bringing into existence a good amateur orchestra associated with the chorus. Finally, the veteran, Dr. Coward, to whom I have put a general question as to the present popularity and also the standard of choral singing, says : " There is more choral singing and better now than ever." He conducts five societies (at Sheffield, Leeds, Huddersfield, Hull, and Derby). The audiences everywhere are excellent. At Huddersfield there is a " waiting list " of 170 would-be subscribers who at present cannot be accommodated. I think this very great choral conductor is right when he adds, " Wherever and whenever you deliver the goods you get increasing support."

KREISLERIANA

I. The Fiddler's Repertory

IN London music, as I write this, Kreisler is the
hero of the moment. He is so popular that
within a few hours of the announcement of one of
his recitals there appears the notice " All seats sold,"
and when the recital takes place the time spent in
applauding the playing amounts to an appreciable
proportion of the time spent in the concert-hall. A
few thoughts on Kreisler and his art seem, then, to
be called for ; they shall take the form of a candid
personal expression.

Our debt to Kreisler was put to me the other day
by a violinist in something like these words : " Prior
to Kreisler, if a violinist had ' technique ' he often
lacked ' warmth ' ; if he had ' warmth ' he lacked
' technique.' But Kreisler had both. He gave recitals
in London in 1901, and at first few people went to
them. Gradually, but pretty quickly, he made his
position, and the old idea that ' technique ' and ' feeling ' were antagonistic was killed. The foundation of
Kreisler's reputation was neither that he was a techni-
cian nor an emotionalist, but that he was *everything*.
Refer to the Press of twenty years ago and you will
constantly find in the criticism of a violinist the phrase,

' As usual with these so highly technically accomplished violinists, the playing was very cold.' The violinist-technician was then at the zenith of his prosperity. Kreisler beat him at his own game, and at the same time turned the game into a work of art." I gladly admit the justice of this appreciation, and if in what follows I seem to make still further demands on this great player, I must not be understood as depreciating the value of what he has already done for us.

The first question I have to ask is this : Cannot Kreisler do something to help us to widen the violinist's repertoire ? I know that this repertoire is of necessity somewhat restricted. But our public performers seem to me to narrow down unnecessarily the collection from which they choose the pieces they play to us. To take a few examples, why always the Chaconne ? Bach wrote six suites and partitas, comprising over two dozen movements. The Chaconne is merely one of these movements. Recently Kreisler played it on a Wednesday, Czaplinski on the following Monday, and Losowsky on the previous Wednesday. There seems to be an idea that every violinist must challenge public criticism with the Chaconne, so that it has become with the big public as much " The " Chaconne as a certain piano piece has become " The " Prelude. (I will return to the Chaconne in a moment.) Similarly violinists, when they play Beethoven, too generally play the Kreutzer Sonata. Kreisler has not lately played us any Beethoven sonatas, but if he does so I should hope to find him deliberately neglecting the over-played Kreutzer, and giving

us instead, perhaps, one of the three in Op. 30
—preferably the great C minor.[1] There are ten
Beethoven sonatas for violin and piano, but the public
must be getting the impression that there is only one.
Then what about Mozart? Pachmann has shown us
that there are Mozart piano sonatas which sound
almost childish as played by the rank-and-file pianist,
but which are really capable of being made surpassingly
beautiful. Are there any of the neglected forty-two
Mozart violin and piano sonatas which Kreisler, with
his great influence, could restore to the repertoire?
So far I have merely spoken of the older classics.
But what of the modern classics? And what of the
younger composers who are trying to get a footing?
Are any of these worthy of Kreisler's help? My
suggestion is that the violin repertoire, like the piano
repertoire, is always, by some mysterious law of
nature (*human* nature), tending to dwindle, and that
nothing but the efforts of a few really great artists
can check this tendency.

Further, the power Kreisler wields is not merely of
life but of death. Complementary to the duty of
planting is the one of weeding. There are some pieces
the playing of which has become traditional amongst
the great teachers and players. One of these is the
Viotti Concerto in A minor. Lately I spoke of
the slow movement of this as "a poor sentimental
hymn-tune." Now a hymn-tune is a most difficult
thing to judge. You have, perhaps, grown up with

[1] A day or two after this was written, a further Kreisler
programme was announced. It included Tartini's hackneyed
" Devil's Trill " and the " Kreutzer."

it, and it is incrusted with associations. There is, perhaps, some tune you *know* to be contemptible but cannot *realize* to be such ; you " know " because years of musical experience have brought you powers of criticism, but you cannot " realize " because it was the first tune you ever heard, and you were lulled to sleep with it every night. You reverence it and dwell fondly upon it and its associations in your quiet moments, but, if you are an organist, you do not help to make it known to a new generation. Now associations almost like these may cling, in the mind of a man like Kreisler, to such a movement as that I have mentioned. Perhaps he first heard it when at the age of seven he studied with Hellmesberger at Vienna (the youngest child ever to enter the Conservatoire there), or when, at the age of twelve, studying under Massart, he gained the gold medal of the Paris Conservatoire against forty competitors, none of whom was less than twenty years of age. But when it comes to making up a public programme, should not these associations be rigorously thrust aside ? Is the vogue of a rather poor piece of music to be perpetuated by the devotion to tradition of a great leader of musical public opinion ? I give here the opening bars of the piece I have mentioned, and I am content to leave decision upon its musical value to the judgment of my readers. But remember that this piece represents a class—the class of violin virtuoso pieces which continue to live on by the possession of no innate musical value, but merely by the opportunity they have always been recognized as offering to the violinist, of exhibiting beautiful tone, or dexterity of bowing, or some other quality which should properly be regarded as but a humble means to the great end of artistic expression.

There is another matter in which Kreisler might help us greatly, and I trust he will do so—the matter of applause. We have a bad habit in this country which Kreisler can help us to kill, that of clapping

in the wrong place. Lately we forced Kreisler to break in this way the performance of the Franck Sonata. But should he allow himself to be thus forced? To an artist of such sincerity our action must have been excessively distasteful, and I suggest that had he not yielded to it, but stood, with impassive face, and bow poised for the opening of the next movement, we should have instantly taken the hint—and next time, perhaps, not required it.

II. " Chaconne à Son Gout "

The jest is not mine ! It occurs in the letter of a
correspondent who, going a little further than I myself
did in discussing a point or two in the Kreisler programmes, says disrespectfully of Bach : " I can't think
why he didn't write a string quartet to be played by
one 'cello and one violin." I can tell this reader the
only reason. Bach never thought of it. As a matter
of fact, the string quartet was not yet an accepted
form of musical art. Haydn was only a youth of
eighteen when Bach died, and Haydn is the father
of all such as handle the four woven strands of the
string quartet. Had Haydn lived a little earlier, or
Bach a little later, we might have had a set of forty-
eight quartets for two players, and the Musicians'
Union, incited by Messrs. Petre and Waldo Warner,
might be vigorously engaged in peacefully picketing
the Æolian Hall to prevent our going to hear Messrs.
Levey and Warwick-Evans give unaided a week's
Bach Quartet Festival, on the lines of the L.S.Q.'s
Annual Beethoven Quartet Festival.

I hope that we who refuse to be carried away by
even Kreisler's playing of the Bach Chaconne are none
of us such superior persons as to profess that we get
no pleasure at all from it. We contend, of course,
that this piece, being but one movement amongst a
great number of similar movements by the same composer, gets a good deal more than its share of performance. That is the first charge on the sheet ;
the second is, that, however enjoyable the piece might
be (heard in a decent moderation), it has the big defect

of not being entirely suited to its medium. For the
foundational law of all musical composition is that
the means and the end shall be suited to one another,
and, indeed, the story of musical progress has largely
been the story of a long-continued attempt to discover
new means of sound-production, and then to work
out the special technique of performance and style
of writing which should show the means employed
to their very best advantage. The stock example of
this process is, of course, the invention of, and gradual
improvement in, the domestic keyed instruments, and
then (later) the development of a style perfectly
suited to their capacities—not a choral style, not
an organ style, a style that would admittedly suit
neither voices nor pipes, but which would perfectly
suit plucked or hammered strings put into vibration
by a fingered keyboard. Our own Elizabethan vir-
ginal composers began this work, and following them
came Couperin in France, Domenico Scarlatti in Italy,
Bach in Germany, and others, down to Chopin and
Scriabin. Similarly, the appropriate style for bowed
string instruments had to be laboriously worked out
by a sort of unorganized syndicate of fiddlers and
composers, and when this was done it still showed
itself clearly enough as a melodic style. A lute could
properly enough play chords, chords might even form
a staple of its stock-in-trade, but for a violin a slow,
singing melody, or a quick, agile running passage, is
the natural thing. Chords we may have, *pizzicato*
passages we may have, but these are but the mustard,
and the slow melody or quicker passage-work is the
beef. For Bach to write his three Sonatas and his

three Suites for Violin alone, or his similar 'Cello pieces, was a splendid thing. He had himself been brought up a fiddler, and he wished, as an interesting problem, to work out the *possibilities* of the instrument, to exploit them to their very last ounce. So great a genius was he that he could even explore these technical possibilities and provide music at the same time. But it could not be his very best music, for what we call " conquering nature " is not flying in the face of her laws, but by patient research coming to understand them more fully and then applying them, and this Bach was surely hardly engaged in doing. So what he produced remained often on the level of a very marvellous *tour de force*, and rarely rose to the higher level of a work of the truest art.

In making this criticism there is some rather singular support to be brought. So many people, in listening to a great fiddler, listen to be astonished by his technique that the sketchy effect of those big chords merely touched by the bow and then abandoned, those harmonies cunningly suggested by the movement of the melody rather than actually sounded, those pretences at a fuller part-writing than is really going on, are accepted uncritically. Bach wrote them, Kreisler plays them, and that is enough for us. If we really *listened*, however (and keen, concentrated attention is, I fear, pretty rare in any concert room), we might become a good deal less complaisant. This brings me to the support I have mentioned. Mendelssohn in 1847 published an edition of this very Chaconne *with added piano part*, and Schumann in 1854 edited the whole six Sonatas and Suites, adding such a part.

" It is incomprehensible," says Schweitzer, " that two such great artists should believe that they were thus carrying out Bach's intention." But we owe the nineteenth-century Bach revival to Mendelssohn, and both he and Schumann were close students and enthusiastic admirers of Bach ; if, then, they, of all men, felt the incompleteness of effect of these attempts to make a melodic instrument do the work of a harmonic and polyphonic one, there is something to be said for those of us to-day who feel it. The Chaconne and its twenty odd companion movements are fine music in their way, but not fiddle music. The very first chord of the Chaconne, which plainly calls for the impact of a hand on a keyboard (see Busoni's piano version, by the way), is a sufficiently convincing quotation. And if Mendelssohn and Schumann, as pianists, are to have their authority on such matters questioned by some violin-playing reader, let me add, for the greater safety of my argument, that, nearer our own days, Wilhelmj himself wrote an accompaniment for the Chaconne. Here, surely, was a confession !

Yet in any bold questioning of the actual effect produced by our great players of to-day in these harmonic-contrapuntal works played on an essentially melodic instrument there is one point which in fairness should be remembered : these players have to conquer difficulties that did not exist, at any rate in such measure, for the fiddlers of Bach's own day. Schweitzer has shown that the flat, mechanically-stretched Italian bow of to-day was little used in Germany during the first half of the eighteenth century. In the old arched bow, still in use there, the tension was effected, not by a screw but by the pressure of the thumb, and the player could at will, as he played, slightly relax the hairs so that they curved over the strings. Chords were thus easy, and this, of course, accounts for the fact that the Germans cultivated polyphonic playing on the violin whilst it remained almost unknown to the Italians. The old bow seems to have lingered longest in northern countries, and the Norwegian Ole Bull is spoken of as the last great representative of the chord-playing school. His bridge was flat, his bow so made that its hair stood off from the stick, and he always spoke of his method as the true and old one. Schweitzer, who is a thorough-paced propagandist for the right ways of doing everything, pleads nobly for a return to the old plan. In order to play these Sonatas as Bach himself did, we " need only file down the arching of the bridge, so as to bring the strings almost level, and use a bow so shaped from nut to point that the hairs can curve towards the stick without touching it." This method has, he says, actually been tried, and he speaks of the resulting tone as a revelation. Which of our great fiddlers will set the example of keeping two violins and two bows in use —one for Bach and one for modern music ?

THE PROMISE OF THE PAST

THIS is the most hopeful moment for British music since the death of Purcell. And that is over two and a quarter centuries ago. My reasons for this assertion are partly based on the special promise of the present and partly on the general promise of the past. Both have to be taken into account. Britain was for long looked upon as the musical " sick man of Europe." Feel the sick man's musical pulse and take his musical temperature and you will have hope of recovery ; inquire into the history of the patient and you will find evidence enough of a sound constitution.

Our past history shows us to be *at heart* a musical nation. You cannot get away from it. It is there in black and white in the history books of Europe, and the stores of British-made musical art in print and in manuscript support the statements of the text-books. To begin with we have the folk-tunes—English, Scottish, Irish and Welsh, Hebridean, Manx, Appalachian, and maritime, love songs, labour songs, drinking songs, hunting songs, fighting songs, cradle songs, sword dances, and morris dances. To me it is amazing that our unlettered peasantry should have produced such a treasure store of lovely melody, much of it as perfect in structure, in its simple way and within its

233

necessarily meagre limits of length, as anything of Mozart or Schubert. The existence of that bulk of beautiful tune is proof enough that the nation's heart beats to music.

But folk-tune is mere melody—a single line of notes, and, after untold centuries of melodic music, the civilized world has developed a harmonic and a contrapuntal art, and for (say) rather over a thousand years has been introducing more and more complex contrapuntal patterns and using ever-increasing harmonic resources. Now, every schoolboy knows (or should know, for it is just as important to find a source of national pride in British music as in English literature or British seamanship), that our own national contribution to the development of harmony and counterpoint has been a big one. Leave out the isolated phenomenon of the thirteenth-century Reading monk's " Sumer is icumen in " and think of Dunstable in the fifteenth century. It was this Englishman who brought to a practical point the efforts of five centuries of striving, showing how could be solved the problem of counterpoint—the artistic weaving together of melodies, each voice with a beautiful thread of sound and all the threads woven into a beautiful fabric. In the fifteenth- and sixteenth-century treatises of Italy, Flanders, Spain, and Germany you may read of Dunstable as the master spirit of the earlier choral age. The choral art of Palestrina, of Bach, and of Handel has an English background.

I pass lightly over the madrigalists and the anthem and service writers of the sixteenth century—famous though they were. Leave their works aside for the moment ; they compare more than favourably with anything the age produced in Italy or elsewhere, but we cannot claim for them that they established a new style or led to a new development such as without them the world might never have seen. With the instrumental works of the century, however, it is different. To the general reader it comes perhaps as a surprise to hear that piano music had ever to be "invented." Yet so it was, and it was we who invented it. The earliest writers for the keyboard instrument (not the piano, but the precursor of the piano, the virginals) had not realized the essential difference between the things fingers on a keyboard can do and those which can only be done effectively by voices in a choir. It was the Elizabethans and early Stuart composers of England who established this differentiation and worked out the problems of the figuration and the forms proper to the medium. A little book of Rubinstein is before me. He took a great interest in the development of keyboard music and gave historical recitals. In this book he talks of the early Italian and French harpsichordists, and adds, " But in England instrumental music, at least for the pianoforte, must have developed itself, since its first beginnings are discovered there." And his six series of Historical Recitals he always opened with some pieces by Bull, Byrd, and Gibbons, for with these men the royal line began. Bach's Suites and Handel's Lessons, Mozart's and Beethoven's Sonatas, Chopin and Schumann and Scriabin are a superstructure gradually erected upon an English foundation.

After the Elizabethans, Purcell—a well-spring of

tune, our national Mozart, a choral genius and an instrumental genius, great in church and great in theatre. Harmony, counterpoint and orchestration may perhaps be taught and learnt. Melody, sheer melody, can only come as a gift of God. And Purcell had that gift. "The Fairy Queen" lately performed at Cambridge is nothing but a string of about fifty tunes spread over an evening and interspersed with mangled Shakespeare. And the tunes never pall. Purcell's touch is sure, his instinct unerring.

I am not clear as to Purcell's influence upon the development of the art, as distinct from his own contribution of a mass of fine music of very varied kind. I do not know that the point has ever yet been fully worked out ; Purcell research has gone on but slowly, and Purcell literature is confined to a few review articles and two books, neither of more than about a hundred pages, as against the hundreds of books on Wagner and on Shakespeare. We can see that he influenced Handel's choral writing. Corelli, we are told, was amongst his greatest admirers, so perhaps he influenced the development of the classic school of string writers. But whatever the extent of his influence, he was, in himself, a great man.

After Purcell comes the slump. Why and how has been much debated. The greatest cause is probably a social one. The time had arrived for the development of the Symphony. We had no orchestras save in London, whereas the German States had an abundance of petty Courts, each with its Kapellmeister and its orchestra. Music was not yet a democratic art. It still needed royal and aristocratic support. Roughly speaking, you can only get your little crop of geniuses if you have a big and well-tilled field under musical cultivation—or rather, a number of experimental farms in which new plans may be tried. Opportunity makes the composer, and we had no opportunity. That is only one cause, amongst several, but it is a big one, and there is a lesson for the twentieth century in our musical failure of the eighteenth and nineteenth.

We are too ready to forget what we did succeed in during those centuries. How many people, for instance, remember that the Irishman Field invented Chopin's Nocturnes for him? How many people think of the eighteenth-century English glee as a peculiarly national possession of some value? How many people know any of the eighteenth-century chamber compositions? Still, relatively, in the eighteenth century we failed and for a century and three-quarters we lagged far behind the Viennese school and, later, the German Romantics.

The pity of it is that the period in which we lagged was precisely the period which provided the music people know well to-day—music that is neither so old as to seem archaic to unaccustomed ears or so new as to seem freakish. Hence the tradition that we are an unmusical nation—even *the* unmusical nation. Yet in choral counterpoint and in keyboard composition we had previously laid the very foundation of modern musical art. The successes of the fifteenth, sixteenth, and seventeenth centuries I look upon as essential, the failures of the eighteenth and nineteenth as accidental, and as due to causes lying largely outside the realm of art and within that of sociology. And the successes would not have been possible had we been at heart an unmusical nation. All this is an old tale, but it needs telling and re-telling, not so much that the Briton may feel conscious pride in his musical history as that he may acquire unconscious dignity and independence and cast off his fatal self-depreciation.

I. Back to School

YOUNG Adolphus is soon to go back to school, and at the breakfast table the burning question is revived as to whether he is to learn music. You put down your newspaper with a natural impatience at the interruption, and try to decide offhand what shall be done. The affair cannot be so quickly settled. This is an important matter to Adolphus, and deserves a little cool thought on the part of his father.

Now what is your difficulty? The boy wants to learn music and you hesitate. Why? Expense? Or you fear it will take his mind off his other studies? Or it may interfere with his games? The last of these fears you may dismiss without further waste of time. In no school nowadays is anything whatever allowed to interfere with games. As for " his other studies," education is a matter not merely of learning this subject or that, but of developing the soul ; and if your boy's soul cries out for music dare you deny it to him? It may be your son needs music to bite his mental and spiritual gums upon just as your neighbour's boy needs mathematics or classics, or modern languages, or science. And as for the expense, whatever that may amount to, you are not going to risk the reproaches of your son in after-life because, through your saving ways, he is missing what his instinct tells him ought to have become one of the keen delights of his life. So that is settled, and we need say no more about it ?

But, on the other hand, perhaps the difficulty is that Adolphus does *not* want to learn music, and you want him to do so. Now do not be guilty of the folly of " In later life, my boy, you'll thank me for insisting." That is the way they talked to you in your young days, but it isn't done now. Besides, you cannot " insist " on a boy's learning music. You can insist on his taking lessons, but that is altogether another thing. Believe me, no boy learns music unless he is keen on it. You may take a boy to the piano, but you cannot make him practise. For " practice " (that is, the practice that brings any sort of perfection) is a matter less of the fingers than of the mind and heart. But perhaps you are blessed beyond the common measure in having a quite improbably dutiful son. Very well, then, you can rely on his trying, though against his will. But if after two or three terms of obedient lesson-taking and prac- tising he still wants to " chuck music," let him. You will do no good to him or to music by using force. You cannot make boys musical by acts of parental authority. Remember old Keate at Eton, in his scripture lesson : " ' Blessed are the pure in heart.' You hear that, boys ? Be pure in heart—or I'll *flog* you ! "

If the boy does want to learn, and you agree, what instrument is he to choose ? " Piano, of course ! " But why " of course " ? Music is not synonymous with piano, though the brass plate we see on the door of the

" Teacher of Singing and Music " suggests it (reflecting, by the way, at the same time upon the value of the vocalism to be acquired within). What are your other children learning ? Piano, " of course." But you do not want five or six pianists in one house, do you ? If you get them I will tell you what will happen. Dorothy will play better than the others (necessarily better than any of the boys, because at her school they give far more time to it than at theirs, and in every way take it more seriously), and in a few years the piano-playing of your household will fall into Dorothy's hands ; she will become a swollen-headed domestic monopolist of the tonal art and all the others will drop their " music," feeling that it is not music enough. Is not that natural ? Have two pianists in the family if you like, for the sake of enabling you and your family to make acquantance with Beethoven's symphonies and overtures, and the rest of the standard classical orchestral stuff in the quite effective form of piano duets. But you need also (at the least) a violinist and a 'cellist. I know the counter arguments—all of them. One is this—the pianist acquires perforce a comprehensive understanding of the art, whereas other instrumentalists, playing but a single line of notes, get but a partial understanding ; his study therefore is in a fuller sense that of " music " than is theirs. But, on the other hand, you have nowadays got to be jolly good as a pianist for your playing to be welcome (and this is one reason why seventy-five per cent. of those who learn the instrument drop it entirely), whereas if you can play passably on one of the other instruments you are acceptable in the making of ensemble music, " chamber " and orchestral. And the

pleasure of ensemble playing is great : here is at once a
form of art and a variety of sport.

Not long ago, I spent a night at an inn on the
borders of Italy and Switzerland. I saw lying there a
piano, two violins, a guitar, a mandoline, and I forget
what other instruments. There were six children in
that innkeeper's family, and each played something.
In the evening there dropped off the train the two
Tagliatelli brothers, of Modena, working their way home
from Northern Switzerland by means of their art. You
have heard these musicians perhaps at some restaurant
in Northern Europe. One plays (with a masterly
technique, and a perfect sense of rhythm and nuance) a
developed form of accordion ; the other ably supports
him on the double bass. The combination is not un-
pleasing, and the performers modestly tell me in confidence that their artistry in the accompaniment of the
dance has been recognized on certain rare occasions by
so high a fee as twenty francs apiece per evening.
Arrived at our inn these musicians at once began to entertain us, and one after another of our young amateurs
took up his or her instrument and joined the professionals, putting it down from time to time to take a hand
(and a foot) with the general company. Sometimes
one of our players would even transfer from one instrument to another, for these are accomplished young
people. I own I looked upon this mountain family with
admiration and agreed with them that they had done
wisely in providing themselves with so perfect a resource
for the long evenings of their extended winter.

Convinced by my arguments you still worry over one
question. Will Adolphus get such teaching and make

such progress as will justify your expenditure? That I cannot promise you, but I will give you a private tip that may aid you to help Adolphus's teacher to do the sensible, practical things and leave the others unattempted. I know personally a good many of those public-school music masters and am able to say (with almost official authority, for I have once occupied for one honourable year the position of President of their Union) that if they were able to feel that they were supported by intelligent parents, who would trust them to teach music rather than " pieces," they could do a great deal better work and, putting it down on that commercial basis to which every argument is necessarily depressed to-day, give you better value for money in times when parenthood itself seems so wildly extravagant a luxury.

II. THE CHILD AND THE GRAMOPHONE

A few years since, studying musical educational conditions in America during a short visit there, I crossed the Charles River that sunders Boston from Cambridge, took a trolly car to the famous Longfellow House, and walked along to the wooden mansion which, next to the White House itself, was perhaps the most frequent objective of the inquiring traveller and the interviewing journalist. Its master, President Eliot, then over eighty years of age, had spent nearly fifty of those years in control of Harvard, and had seen all the developments in educational thought and practice which half a century at that busy period of the world's progress had brought with it. In a very interesting conversation he gave me some of his conclusions, and one of these was that music was, as an element in education, of far greater value than had even yet been realized. " A good music school," he said (I give his actual words as I noted them at the time), " gives an admirable training of eye, ear, and hand, and imparts an accurate and faithful use of all the senses. It is through a training of the senses to a high degree that the human race has attained all its most valuable knowledge, including the applied sciences of the last hundred years. Music is not physical training alone, but also intellectual and moral training. . . . It is by a wonderful co-ordination of the senses, acting in common with the imagination and the reasoning power, that the greatest discoveries of the human mind are brought out and put to do the work of humanity. Music is not a mere recreation, a refined hobby. Actually it takes its place as an education—as a means of developing the human child, of drawing out latent powers and enabling him to make the best of himself. So far from being a special subject, to be reserved for the children of the well-to-do, music is one of the very best things for children who will leave school at fourteen. A musical training is the child's *birthright*, though often he may at present be deprived of it. Nothing will more perfectly cultivate the human spirit."

Now President Eliot had a feeling of urgency in this matter that we here do not fully share ; at that time there were eighteen million children in the schools of the United States, and of these only five million were receiving any kind of systematic musical training. This proportion is immensely lower than with us, for throughout all our elementary schools and most of our secondary schools some systematic musical training *is* given, and our problem is merely—can we improve our system ? If our training does not tend to the production of the humane results promised by President Eliot, then our system is wrong somewhere. If it is not " an education —a means of developing the human child, of drawing out latent powers," an opportunity of " cultivating the human spirit," it is somewhere incomplete, and this, I think, is actually the case.

The lack in our school musical training, as I have said elsewhere and often, has long been just this—it has not brought the child into touch with master-pieces. It would be deplorable if the encouragement that is now being given to the teaching of what is called " Appreciation of Music " were to lead to any neglect of the teaching of class singing ; but class singing, as we have in practice found, is not in itself enough, for to limit a child's school acquaintance with music to what his own ear-mind can grasp and his own throat reproduce is cruelly to narrow his outlook. Yet until a few years ago there was no escape from this limitation. You could not bring an orchestra into the school, nor often even a string quartet. The school piano was not a good one and the school pianist worse. In the best secondary schools, with their full material equipment and highly trained staff, some " appreciation " work could be done, but the mass of the population, as we know, passes not through the secondary schools, but through the elementary schools, and what was wanted, if we were to develop " appreciation " on a large, popular scale, was an adequate and easy means

of performance of great music in schools where the
equipment was necessarily slender, and the staff did not
include any body of musical specialists. This means
we now find in the gramophone, and I, for one, welcome
it heartily. With the gramophone we can at least do
something towards giving the child what Professor Eliot
has sanely called his " birthright." We can make Bach
and Beethoven and Elgar quite familiar figures to him ;
the performance of the best music can become one of the
customary features of school life.

A correspondent in " The Times Educational Supplement " lately pleaded for " the occasional performance
of good music in the schools." He was too modest ;
we should aim not at the occasional, but at the regular.
A provincial paper, showing real understanding of
present-day conditions, has spoken as follows :

It is now possible to bring the work of the greatest
performers and best orchestras into every classroom.
Thus, school-children would be able to learn as much
about a Beethoven Symphony as they now do about
the Wars of the Roses. After all, it is as important
that a boy should know and should learn to admire
the C minor Symphony as it is that he should know
about the military exploits of Marlborough. It is
more important that he should learn to know the
art songs of Schubert and Schumann, by hearing
the most able recitalists sing them, than it is that he
should learn by heart " Excelsior " ; and more important that he should know something about the
" William Tell " overture than he should know that
William Tell once pierced with an arrow an apple
placed on a boy's head. And about next in importance, from the point of view of culture, to appreciating

good syntax, is to know that a good musical work, like a well-written essay, is built by logical arrangement of orderly phrases and sections.

We may not attach quite so much importance to a knowledge of the once famous " William Tell " overture as does the " Huddersfield Examiner," but the general idea is sound, and with the help of the Gramophone the work of Beethoven may be made as familiar as the doings of Buonaparte, and the idea of the logical development of a piece of music as familiar as that of the logical development of a piece of prose. " Music has become to us an unknown tongue," said Sir Henry Hadow lately. " For a very large number of people, to go to a concert, and especially a concert of modern music, is exactly like going to see a play in a language they do not understand." Our business is to make that language so familiar that it is understood by all. Our admirable Walford Davies, now Director under the National Council of Music of Wales, has said that an expression he often hears is, " I am passionately fond of music, but cannot make head or tail of it." The only means of making the " head and tail " of music clear to the big public is to give them frequent hearings of it when they are young.

III. " AN UNMITIGATED CURSE "

Mr. Holst and Mr. Bliss have lately used strong words about a familiar feature in our musical life. Examinations Mr. Holst described as " a stimulant or form of drug, which left the individual most concerned in a state of subsequent relapse," adding that

" the joy of competing was far too often a substitute
for the subtle joy of music *per se*, which thereby suffered accordingly." Mr. Bliss went further, roundly
condemning all examinations as "an unmitigated
curse." In my opinion Mr. Bliss is wrong. Mr.
Holst, however, is partly right. There are schools in
this country where to learn music is but to proceed
from one examination to another, practising nothing
that is not in the year's examination syllabus. This
is, at the best, a form of sport, and a poor one at that.
On the other hand, there are schools where the examination is taken in the pupil's stride, causing no devia-
tion from a sound course of training, offering to the
pupil a little occasional " stimulant " that is not at all
undesirable, and affording the parent some assurance
that steady progress is being made. In our grandparents' days musical examinations were unknown
(save only those for University degrees). But our
grandparents spent their music practice time upon
"Warblings at Eve," " The Mocking Bird," " The
Battle of Prague," and " The Maiden's Prayer," and
the disappearance of material of that kind from the
school musical curriculum is largely due to the higher
standard of taste and of execution that were brought
in by this very examination system.

But there is one abuse which persists, and rarely is
any voice raised against it—public examination by
private bodies. If I, living in Bloomsbury, were to set
up a University of Bloomsbury, and create Mus. Bacs.
and Mus. Docs., the Government would stop me. If my
baker or candlestick-maker were to set up in Bloomsbury an " Imperial College of Music," and grant diplo-

mas of A.I.C.M. and F.I.C.M., and certificates, not a Whitehall dog would bark. And, in fact, within almost a stone's throw of my house are several musical examining institutions with not a bit more status and not a bit more certainty of good faith than the presence on their " boards " of such diligent tradesmen would give them. These institutions examine throughout the country and throughout the Empire. They are usually (but not always), for financial security, limited companies, printing the " Ltd.," however, in so small a type as to be virtually invisible. In style of title they are undistinguishable from the genuine institutions, and, in fact, they are pretty generally confused with these by pupils, parents, and less educated music-teachers. I have upon my desk as I write a photograph, cut from a local paper, of two sisters of eleven and twelve years respectively, each wearing the cap and gown of one of these " colleges," and each entitled to place after her name on a nice brass door plate " letters " which will inevitably be confused by the local public with those indicating possession of a diploma from the Royal Academy of Music or the Royal College of Music. This one quite unauthorized institution grants every half-year 600 to 700 such " professional diplomas," and the certificates for its examinations of pupil grade are given in thousands or tens of thousands. Incidentally, there are one or two of these bodies whose prospectus offers you a professional diploma and " letters " without examination—but not without fee !

The appearance upon the examiners' list of such an institution of the names of musicians possessing

genuine University degrees is no guarantee of good
faith. Otherwise honest men will yield to inducements
to accept examinerships in a bogus " college " when
approached in a moment of financial pressure, and
once in the system, escape is difficult. Equally, the
appearance of the names of peers and bishops upon
a prospectus offers no security. When approached
tactfully in what is called " the interests of education," no benevolent bishop or patriotic peer will be
so impertinent as to inquire into the standing of those
who approach him. The resounding title, " Imperial
College of Music," which I have suggested as that of
an institution which I mean to found when I have
lost most of my money and all of my morals, will, in
itself, be accepted as a guarantee of academic respec-
tability by the Earl of Pudsey and the Bishop of
Chowbent just as readily as by some cottage parent
in those places. I shall secure a president and vice-
president without difficulty, and both "patrons "
and patrons.

" Truth " has, off and on, for thirty years, called
attention to this evil. Here is an extract from an
article of June 7, 1922 (readers interested should obtain
a copy of the issue, which gives names and particulars
of many of the bogus " colleges," " academies," and
" conservatories," and should also obtain " Musical
Examinations—Dubious " (Curwen, 1s. 6d.) :

Every little music teacher who has been unable
to secure a diploma from one of the recognized examining bodies in the country has to find some means
of meeting the competition of those more fortunate,
and to the uninstructed public one string of letters

following the name is very much like another. Nor is the provision of advertising material for music teachers the only business function the musical milliners perform. Every little private academy for young ladies teaches music as a profitable " extra." Parents like to have some assurance that they are getting what they pay for, and the certificate issued by a body with a high-sounding name appears to be a guarantee that the money paid for teaching Jane to strum on the piano has not been wasted. The publication of the names of their offspring in local newspapers as having passed the examination of this, that, or the other " college " or " academy," maybe with " honours," also flatters parental pride. Thus the musical milliners do a huge business in examinations. They largely exist to cater for the demand for pieces of paper and parchment which are so useful to the lesser middle-class schools of the country. . . . That their efforts do nothing except retard real musical education matters not to them. Business is business, and the *raison d'être* of the musical milliner is to sell his wares, whether of paper, stuff, or silk.

A useful step taken recently was the definite exclusion of the advertisements of these bogus institutions from the pages of all the more important members of the musical Press. Moreover, all of them are, of course, refused recognition in any way by the official, Government-founded, Teachers' Registration Council. If you ask me why the governing bodies of the genuine and national musical institutions do not take active steps to suppress a nuisance and a danger (and at the same time a gross injustice to their own graduates), I can only reply that I am as puzzled as you.

"IMPERSONAL TRUTH" IN CRITICISM

A VERY distinguished composer lately wrote to me begging me to abandon the first person singular in my writing. "We stand," he says, "in such great need, at the moment, of musical criticism with the weight of simple impersonal truth behind it," and he sympathetically adds, "Of course I know it is the last achievement of noble minds, and very hard to attain," humbly concluding his letter—"Your forgiveness, please!" There is nothing to forgive, but, on the contrary, matter for thanks, for my correspondent has given me an easy opening for the discussion of a vital matter that has long been in my mind.

Some time ago another friend, who edits a London paper, showed me, who happened to drop in upon him in his office, a letter he had just received from a reader and the reply he had sent to it. They ran as follows :

From the Reader.—"Dear Sir, Why do your dramatic and music critics always write ' I ' in their articles and criticism ? "
From the Editor.—"Dear Sir, Because that is precisely what we pay them to do."

And there, we may suppose, the matter dropped. The responsibility for what the reader probably con-

252

sidered a piece of blatant journalistic swank on the part of the critics was shifted on to the right shoulders, which could well bear it. But why should it ever be thought egotistical to say "I think," "I feel," "My opinion is"? Surely the true egotism lies in the bolder practice of saying "The Symphony is a bad one," "Mr. X's interpretation of the sonata is wrong." Such dogmatism is unjustifiable, for the attainment of "simple impersonal truth" is not merely "the last achievement of noble minds" (as my friend the composer rather grandiloquently puts it); it is an unimaginable achievement for any human mind, noble or not; to arrive at it is not merely "hard," but impossible. Outside the realm of mathematics no man is justified in saying "This is truth"—and even there some passing Einstein may throw in a word that will in a moment remove the justification. Certainly in the criticism of art not only the wise but also the truly modest man is, paradoxically, the very man who always says "I." Those of us, then, who are allowed or requested, by very sensible editors, to sign or initial all we write, and even to use the first person singular, are the truly modest members of the corps of critics—modest, and (here's another paradox!) proud of our modesty!

In speaking of the impossibility of attaining "simple impersonal truth" do I seem to be depreciating the value of musical criticism? I hope not. I do not intend that. I am merely suggesting that the worth of a piece of music or of a performance is as much a matter of opinion as (say) the interpretation of a passage of Scripture or an Act of Parliament. That

" misguided monarch " who never appears in person
in the " Gondoliers," but whose change of theological
opinions lies at the back of its whole plot, " abandoned
the creed of his forefathers and became a Wesleyan
Methodist of the most bigoted and persecuting type,"
and, I have no doubt, adduced as the grounds of his
conversion some of the very texts which his own
Grand Inquisitor had intended to bring against him
in confutation. Paul and Apollos, Luther, Calvin,
Savonarola, Laud, Wyclif, Wesley, Dean Inge, and
Dr. Orchard—the list can be extended indefinitely of
men of piety and learning basing their arguments on
the same documents and arriving at different conclusions. Where amongst these is the " simple impersonal truth " ? Are you bold enough to lay your
hand on the shoulders of one of them and say he alone
has it ? Or turn from theology to law : where is the
judge whose verdicts may never be overturned on
appeal, and then overturned again, until at last a
masterful House of Lords (not, I hope, regarding itself
as the mouthpiece of " simple impersonal truth," but
mercifully considering that there must be an end
somewhere, even to litigation) gives its final decision ?
Then where shall we look for the so-much-to-be-
desired " simple impersonal truth " ? In Harley
Street, perhaps ? Try it ! If sufficiently wealthy
you will find it an instructive way of passing an afternoon to call with your guineas and some slight, out-
of-the-way ailment at six consecutive doors. This
" simple impersonal truth " is indeed a very great
myth. The only simple impersonal truth with
which I in my lifetime have ever met is the simple

impersonal truth that simple impersonal truth does not exist.

The liability to error in musical criticism does not, then, mean that musical criticism is valueless, any more than medical, legal, or theological opinion is valueless. It only means that it should be written with caution and read with discretion. There are critics and critics, as there are theologians and theologians, lawyers and lawyers, doctors and doctors. The best critic, I take it, is he whose native discrimination and plain common sense are the strongest, whose knowledge and experience are the widest, whose sincerity is the most unvarying, and whose ability is most developed to put on paper plainly and attractively what he really thinks, and to set you thinking for yourself. Whether he uses the first person singular, or the first person plural, or (in rather cowardly fashion, I think) tries to evade the charge of egotism by the awkward use of "one," or perhaps, cunningly avoids pronouns altogether, read him with an open but agile mind. He is putting before you nothing which it is safe to take as "simple impersonal truth," but merely his own opinion for your consideration, and this opinion is unavoidably biased by his temperament, his upbringing, his education, his environment, and even the state of his liver on the night when he heard what he is describing or wrote what he wrote about it. I have previously pleaded that all newspaper criticism should be signed—in fairness to composer, performer, reader, and the writer himself. I am not sure that I went far enough. Perhaps, for complete safety, it should always open somewhat thus: "The

opinions of myself, A—— B——, upon C—— D——'s
new string quartet, being sound of mind and body,
but after spending an afternoon in filling in my income
tax return," or this : " The views of myself, E——
F——, upon Madame G—— H——'s singing, being
well in pocket, but suffering from a touch of tooth-
ache," or thus : " The criticism of I—— J—— upon
K—— L——'s piano playing, written after dining
with some friends not unwisely but quite well enough."
And everything the critic wrote should, of course,
conclude with the cautious words " Subject to correc-
tion or alteration upon a second hearing."

SHALL WE RECONSIDER WOLF?

THIS is not an attack on Hugo Wolf; it is not so to be thought of, much less is it so to be quoted. It is simply a plea for a reconsideration of Wolf's work, with a view to a possible adjustment of his position. Every great writer is in need of re-appraisement from time to time, but most of all the highly productive writer, in whose case there is always the danger that his few best things, becoming the best known, will be taken as the measure of his everyday production, and create for him a reputation that will then blind people to the weaknesses of his less truly successful work. An obvious illustration outside music is the case of Burns. I open the volume quite at random and find myself looking at the epitaph that ends the " Elegy on Captain Matthew Henderson ":

> But now his radiant course is run,
>   For Matthew was a bright one;
> His soul was like the glorious sun,
>   A matchless, Heav'nly Light, man."

And you might open the volume again and again and find for a time nothing better. To hear a Scot talk on January 25 you would think that the whole of Burns was the purest gold. I suggest that musicians to-day, and especially singers, talk of Wolf as many a Scotsman talks of Burns. Wolf is the perfect

257

song writer, they say. He surpasses Schubert and leaves Brahms very far behind. I would almost defy my readers to find me amongst all the critical writings of the last ten years a sentence of downright blunt dispraise, such as every composer who has ever lived has surely sometimes earned.

Of Wolf's songs two-hundred-and-sixty or two-hundred-and-seventy have, I think, been published. Many of these were very quickly written. Between February and May, 1888, he wrote forty-three of the Mörike settings ; between October and February, 1889, fifty Goethe settings ; soon after this he set forty-four poems from the Spanish Song Book, and then twenty-two from the Italian Song Book. " For that was how he composed. He would sit down to a volume of poems and work at white heat, flinging off songs day after day, hardly stopping to eat or sleep until the fit of inspiration had passed, when he would relapse into a fit of despondency and lethargy that lasted until the next furious outburst." Nearly all the songs of his that we hear to-day were written in the years 1888 to 1891. They were literally dashed down on paper, sometimes two in one day. Can they, then, all be so perfectly shaped as we have been told ? Can the very choice of poems set have been quite so unerring as we are asked to believe ? Is not a little inquiry justified ? And is there any way of pursuing such an inquiry fairly but by taking the composer's whole output, and with a firm resolution to be biased neither in favour of it nor against it by the unlimited praise of which it has been the subject, to go carefully through it, every bit, song by song ?

Let us make a beginning with the famous Mörike
set. I think that in its first pages it suggests to us
the necessity of a sifting process. " The Convalescent's
Song of Hope " opens the volume. Frankly, is it
quite worth the unqualified praise it gets ? I suggest
that by the time it has passed into its second page it
has dropped into the conventional German *Lieder*
style, and that the concluding lines are perilously near
our British " ballad " level. " The Boy and the Bee "
comes next, with its second-half-of-the-Prom.-pro-
gramme tale of a little house on a vine-clad mountain,
and a bee buzzing around the flowers, to whom the
singer tells how his dearest, too, has a garden and some
bees, and asks tidings of her. We will not blame
Mörike for the English version of his poem :

> What knows a maid of loving
>   That is almost a schoolgirl yet ?
> The dear little maid you're wooing
>   Is still a mother's pet.

"Mein   Lieb hat einen Gar - ten, da steht ein hübsches Immenhaus:
"My   dear - est has a gar - den, therein one can a bee-hive see:

But is not this sort of subject, in the wholesale
(as we get it in Mörike and Wolf), just a little trivial

and even mawkish ?   And does not the music too well match the words ?

We now come to " Just ere the Dawn of Day." I suppose it is irreverent of me to call this dry.   We pass on to the " Huntsman's Song," the opening of which I dare to suggest is in the worst stick-in-the-mud Sunday-school hymn-book style of harmonization :

Zier - lich ist   des Vo - gels Tritt im Schnee, wenn   er
Dain - ti - ly   the bird doth tread the snow, when   on

Follows the neatly managed, slightly humorous, and very popular " The Drummer," and then comes the " Song to Spring," which begins like one of those Franz Abt or second-rate Mendelssohn songs formerly beloved of girls' school singing teachers (conventional harmonic progressions and obvious melody), and ends with a page of incredibly banal piano strumming of this sort :

Have I made out a case for a reconsideration of Wolf? Then let us reconsider him! We shall, of course, find some great songs, but already we can see that we shall also find some weak ones. How will Wolf at last emerge from our candid questionings? We shall probably pronounce of him as Watts-Dunton did of Burns: " Although Burns, like so many other fine poets, has left behind him some poor stuff, it would be difficult to exaggerate . . . "—and so on to the laudation. We shall praise Wolf, then, but I think we shall begin our praise with " although." And the strange thing is that we shall be almost the first to do this!

SANTLEY

THE recent death of Sir Charles Santley is not so
much the breaking of a link with the past as
the removal of a link that had long ago become detached
from its chain. For at the time of his death Santley
was eighty-eight years old, and the great names pro-
fessionally associated with his have almost passed out
of current conversation. When I was listening to
" Faust " at Covent Garden a year or two since, it
suddenly burst upon my recollection with a shock
of surprise that we had still living amongst us the
singer who had first in England (nearly sixty years
before) sung the part of Valentine, and for whom
Gounod (in 1864) wrote the solo, " Even bravest
heart."

The facts of Santley's career were recorded, at the
time of his death, with considerable detail in every
paper in the country. Especial interest, I think,
attached to the obituary notice in the " Daily Telegraph," written by the veteran Joseph Bennett, who
predeceased the subject of his article by eleven years.
Santley was a Liverpool boy. He began to sing early
(at fifteen—too early, one would have thought). At
first he sang but locally, and in a small way. He was
apprenticed to the provision trade, and when out of
his indentures became a bookkeeper. At last, encour-

aged by his father, he set off for Italy, with £40 in his
pocket, to return some years later " without a penny,
and with his portmanteau in pawn." His early reception here was not very cordial, and he was willing to
take part of the blame for this, admitting that on
occasion he had not sung well. There is encouragement for the younger generation in the story of Santley's early struggles and ultimate success. He knew
what it was to " wander from one agent's office to
another, to be told that I had not sufficient voice to
sing in a theatre, that my style of singing was not
adapted to the exigencies of the public taste, and that
it was necessary to have the voice of a bullock and
sing like a butcher." And his book, " The Art of
Singing and Vocal Declamation," was, as he said in
his preface, written " to warn those who are about to
enter the arena of what they will have to encounter,
and, at the same time, to encourage them to fight
valiantly." " The Art of Singing " is still obtainable,
and, though in some ways a rather naïve production,
it contains much that is of value to the student. Other
literary works were " Student and Singer " and the
volume of " Reminiscences."

Like others of his generation, Santley held a little
kindly contempt for the vocal methods of to-day.
There was too much of the get-rich-quick about them
for him, and he deplored the lack of patience that
pushed young singers into an early appearance. Like
his contemporaries, again, he complained that " most
of the composers of vocal music of our own day have
either been ignorant of, or have paid no attention to,
the capabilities of the human voice," with the result,

as he thought, of excessive " wear and tear " and early
decline of singing power. When Santley was eighty-
three I used much persuasion (applied through his
close friend, Mr. J. L. Levien, hon. secretary of the
Philharmonic Society) to induce him to submit to
the visit of an interviewer from a paper I then edited,
" The Music Student." The interview was duly
written, set in type, and approved, but had, at the
last moment, to be withheld. Sir Charles took fright.
He feared that the views he had expressed would lead
to correspondence and controversy, to which, at his
advanced age, he felt unequal. The objection is now
removed. Here is a typical extract. It represents
the view not merely of Santley, but, I think, of any
surviving singers of the Santley period :

" Thirty years ago there was a tradition of singing
and singers. Now singers have lost the ideal of tone.
They don't know what they are aiming for, and ten
to one the teacher can't tell them. Half the stuff
you hear in the concert room isn't singing at all.
Students are told to admire this and the other singer ;
they imitate them, copy their affectations, but the
result is no more singing than the voice of a cow or a
donkey."

Without endorsing all that is there said it may be
sorrowfully admitted that we *are* at present passing
through a bad period in vocalism. We have a number
of singers with the musical temperament and brains,
but comparatively poor natural voices, or voices that
have early lost their " ring." And we have, equally,
singers with voices but without the brains and the

musicianship. The full combination is now decidedly rare :

" When the National Training School of Music (afterwards the Royal College of Music) was first inaugurated, Sir George Grove asked me to come as one of the Singing Professors. I said ' No.'
" ' No ! Why not ? ' he asked.
" ' Because not one in a hundred of your vocal students ought to sing.'
" ' But we have some very good voices there now,' he protested.
" ' Voices—ah, yes ! but you can't make a singer out of a voice alone.' "

One of the outstanding qualities of Santley's singing was clear articulation. He was trained in Italy under a great Italian teacher (Gaetano Neva), but he held a view, contrary to that usual in his time, that Italian was " the most difficult of all the languages generally wedded to music." English, he held, was for the singer " a fine language," but usually spoken and sung in slipshod fashion.

Some of the quainter ideas of Santley are perhaps worth passing mention. He strongly objected to flowers on a platform, as the odour, he said, " made his voice husky even to hoarseness." At the Crystal Palace once, finding the platform lined with hyacinths in full bloom, he insisted upon their removal, " which made George Grove furious, and caused him to declare in a loud voice that it was ridiculous to keep the audience waiting for such nonsensical fads." Yet the " weed " he emphatically approved, and he devoted a whole

chapter in his " Art of Singing " to the narration of
his one-time objection (so strong that when his father-
in-law visited him he made him go into the garden
to smoke), and his later conversion (when the baby
came, " and indigestion and domestic bliss began to
interfere with my work and my temper "). But all
Santley's views, on little things and big, were condi-
tioned by the bearing of the subjects he discussed upon
his art. He felt deeply upon this because it was a
part of his religion. He occupied the last page of
one of his books thus : " EPITAPH : Be true to your
Art, and you shall earn this—*Though your Mortal
Body lies here awaiting the call of the last Trumpet,
your Immortal Soul shall ascend to join the Celestial
Choir in singing the eternal praise of its Creator.*"

CHURCH MUSIC

I. What the Organist Said

THERE is a crisis in English church music. The Cathedrals have insufficient funds to carry on their daily choral services and many have, I believe, already dropped the attendance of the choir at week-day matins. To a greater extent than many people would think the future of British music (in a wide sense of general cultivation and appreciation, especially) depends upon the state of music in the English church. For centuries the church was the training school for the British musician. Dunstable and Byrd and Gibbons and Purcell and all the composers of the three centuries covered by their lifetimes were trained in the church ; right down to Sterndale Bennett and Sullivan our composers have nearly all been cathedral or Chapel Royal choir boys, and, indeed, until the Royal Academy was opened in 1823 systematic training in music was hardly to be had except in the church. The normal career of a musician in this country began by his becoming a cathedral choir boy, then an articled pupil of the organist, and later assistant organist of the cathedral. Say what we like about the narrowness of conception which sometimes resulted, the training, within its limits, was a pretty thorough one.

There is a fine essay by Filson Young (in " More Mastersingers," I think) which draws a most sympathetic picture of the routine of a great cathedral— draws it from the author's memories of his own training under Kendrick Pyne at Manchester. This gives the best idea of the cathedral musical atmosphere with which I have met. To-day all this is threatened. To Londoners it may perhaps not seem to matter a great deal, but in many provincial districts the cathedral is still the centre of musical activity, and a change which will destroy cathedral musical efficiency may be a blow to music.

This was in my mind when I met a cathedral organist the other day and took him to lunch, so that I might question him as to an address on church music he was to give that afternoon to a gathering of London organists. And to my surprise he said never a word about the present discontents, but came down to something so much more fundamental that, before he had done, he had, whilst talking all the time of church music, provided me with a criterion by which I could test any artistic product whatever—the pictures at Burlington House, or the Cavell monument, or the Russian Ballet, as much as the music of Westminster Abbey or a village church. There are some superior musical people about, who, neglectful of all we owe to organists, would consider that " What the organist said is not evidence." But everything this one said was common sense ; there was nothing really new about any of it, but it was all so clearly put that it seems to me very well worth repeating—for the guidance especially of some of our younger

and more thoughtless singers and players and composers.

The first point made was that in church music two
essentials are to be looked for—beauty and expression.
And here, of course, is the trite old truism that applies
to every form of art. Applied to church music it
would abolish at least fifty per cent. (and more likely
seventy-five per cent.) of the music in use. Sir Frederick Bridge said to me the other day, " When I was
a young man I thought everything in the great collections of old Boyce and Arnold was of gospel value ;
now I see that it is only an anthem or service here
or there that is really worth performing ; a few things
are wonderful, the rest is routine stuff." That, I
imagine, is true enough. A church music formula arose
in the sixteenth century and people wrote in it music
that expressed something and music that expressed
nothing, music that was beautiful and music that was
merely respectable and dull. The formula was varied
in the next century, and a slightly different composing-
routine established ; so, too, in the eighteenth century
and in the nineteenth, so that the winnowing fan of
that simple little dual requirement would blow away
chaff in clouds and leave a very tiny heap of grain.
But, it being a much easier thing to test a piece of
music by seeing whether it conforms to a formula
than by really listening to find out whether it has
any beauty of its own and really means something,
and church music publishers and choirmasters and
cathedral precentors and the clergy and their congregations being, on the whole, a herd of unthinking
sheep, a vast accumulation of rubbish has been stored

up that will take a lot of burning when we begin to think a little. And when we do that, not only will our hymn books and anthem books be purged, but we shall set aside a good deal of Mozart and Beethoven and even Bach—to the greater reputation of their names in the next generation. And in that happy day the British National Opera Company's repertory will be a much finer one than it is now, for a more understanding public will leave it free to consult its own (doubtless perfect) taste. As for the songs and piano pieces we see in the music shop windows, it is no exaggeration but a mild understatement if I say that but one in a thousand would survive the obvious test, which, as one would think, every one might constantly apply as the merest matter of course—(a) Is it beautiful? (b) Does it mean something?

Here one is reminded of two types of great singers. There is a famous woman singer whose voice and presence and ability would enable her to popularize any fine song she wished, but who frequently sings music that has no real depth or meaning. And there are three men singers to whom nature has given very imperfect voices, but who choose nothing but stuff that has beauty and meaning and who sing it with brains. Honour to the second type rather than the first. If we cannot have both beauty of voice and expressive force the latter is the more important of the two.

The next great principle my cathedral organist laid down was again a dual one—that of variety plus unity. Unity he called the brain side of church music and variety the spiritual side. Unity is the result of hard practice, variety of personality breaking through this. Such a quality in choral singing as " blend " is an instance of unity, but with it there must be the variety that comes from freedom. There are cathedrals famous for their music that give us merely the product of rehearsal-room drill. Brains have been used, but spirit is stifled. Most of the London musical critics spoke in their various papers of the recent visit of a certain foreign Symphony Orchestra in a way that showed their complete recognition of this principle of balance of two apparently conflicting elements, and you may constantly read remarks about piano recitals that involve its acceptance. Obviously this principle of unity plus variety is very like the principle formerly mentioned of beauty plus expression. I am not sure it does not really come to the same thing.

And connected with those must be, said my friend, also the old admitted principle that art must conceal art. But this, I imagine, when the former principles have been applied, comes about of itself, whether in piano or vocal recital, choral performance, or, whatever it may be. For the art of self-expression covers up the evidence of the art that has been employed to secure beauty.

Another requirement laid down (this time especially of the conductor and choirmaster) was that of being able to control oneself in order that one may then control others. The man who could keep his head during an air raid ought to be able to come into church on a depressing November Sunday morning, pull himself together and carry things through. His choir boys will respond to him more quickly than his

choir men, but both will feel his influence coming
down from the organ loft. The player or singer or
conductor who can only do well when conditions are
perfect will have few opportunities of doing well.
When Ffrangcon Davies was to sing " Elijah," and
the conductor insisted on starting amid the hubbub
of late comers arriving and programme sellers taking
money, he had such self-control that his first few
notes controlled the audience and the hubbub ceased.
Another man would have been disturbed, made a bad
beginning, and perhaps never to the very end of the
oratorio have emerged into the glow of self-expression.
The ability to concentrate on one's work, to control
one's own mood, is of even more value to the pianist
than the ability to play scales at lightning speed.
" Greater is he that ruleth his own spirit than he that
taketh a city."

Lastly (and here is something which elaborated
would become a sermon)—it is no good undertaking
any artistic work whatever unless you have a " sense
of message." So, at least, the organist said. I do
not give his name, for it may be my memory has
in some way misrepresented his views. But he is a
famous North of England organ player and voice
trainer and choral conductor, and there are north-
country readers of this essay who will recognize his
thought and say at once " That's —— ! "

II. SOME CHURCH MUSIC ABROAD

Easter Day in Rome. St. Peter's thronged with a
devout congregation of the faithful, the Pope in person

present, silver trumpets, wonderfully expressive singing
by a highly trained choir of picked voices—that is
the romantic tradition of the Roman Easter in which
from boyhood I have been brought up. I have at
last spent Easter in Rome and the tradition has
crumbled. No overflowing congregation, but an
empty nave, a half-empty choir with a small railed-
off portion occupied by the tiny true congregation,
and behind it a standing group of a few hundred
sightseers walking about and chatting together in
many tongues as Mass was sung by Cardinal Merry
del Val, the clergy and a little group of men and
boys in a side gallery, supported by a small and
inferior organ. About those clergy—they chant
through their noses ; about that choir—it is a crude
little collection of half-trained men and untrained
boys, incapable of singing *a capella* music unless
doubled by an accompaniment ; about that organ—
it is impossible to say with conviction at any moment
whether the player is using its diapasons, its reeds,
or its string stops. And the organ extemporization
before and during the service on Easter Day consisted
of a few loosely strung common chords, unrhythmi-
cally played—our village-organist style.

I was told both before I left England and after I
got to Rome, that I should hear the best music not
at St. Peter's, but at St. John Lateran. I was in the
Lateran one day when they were singing. A little
simply harmonized chant, of the same few notes, was
being repeated over and over again. The tenors were
coarse ; the boys forced their voices ; the whole choir
went out of tune in certain chords whenever they

occurred (yet miraculously regained itself, I admit, and hence did not flatten in the piece as a whole). There seemed to be no standard in church music here, as there seemed to be none at St. Peter's. Italian artistic feeling is very undependable in its working. You find, for instance, in the church decoration everywhere that the loveliest things and the tawdriest are mixed. In this magnificent Lateran church, in addition to the main organ, is in one corner a small one with the plainest red-painted deal-board tribune. No suburban mission church in England would admit such a piece of furniture. Artistic and musical toleration is in Italy miles wider in its scope than with us.

The only good church singing I happened to hear in Rome was at the great Gesù church—the very headquarters of the Jesuit body, where they still show you the room and the relics of their founder, Loyola. Here about twenty men, standing before and facing the altar, conducted by one of their number standing in their midst and beating time, sang some plainly harmonized short pieces with good voices and well-blended tone. It was a pleasure to hear a simple thing so perfectly done.

It is fair to admit that what music I heard I came to in a chance way. More methodical visitors wander round with a little book (in English) " Easter Music in the Churches of Rome," and some of them return to their hotels with tales of " lovely singing." Perhaps these tales are true—but I doubt it. From my own experience I am led to guess that these good people go to Rome with the same romantic ideas as I, but are less willing to readjust them to realities. Almost all my experiences of Italian music have so far been bad. Years ago I heard in Milan Cathedral (Milan, then the vocal training centre of the world !) coarse, nasal singing such as would barely be tolerated by us in a slum church. In St. Mark's, Venice, last summer, on a great feast day, I took up my position amongst the mosaic saints and angels in one of those wonderful galleries, prepared to spend the morning in listening to beautifully sung unaccompanied choral music of the Palestrina period. Here was, I reasoned, one of the very homes of Italian church music at its best— St. Mark's, famous already for its church music in the fifteenth century, with Willaert, and the Gabrielis, Zarlino, and De Rore amongst its musicians in the sixteenth century. Monteverde and Cavalli in the seventeenth, and Browning's Galuppi in the eighteenth. But alas ! the voices were again coarse, and the singing technically imperfect in every possible way ; and, not content with a time-beating choirmaster to keep them together, the choir needed also a blaring organ duplication of all they were doing. I stood there for a quarter of an hour and came away saddened. What is wrong with Italian church music ? Why has its standard gone ? I leave the explanation to others who know the country more intimately than I. But I fear the decadence is of fairly long standing. Dr. Burney, writing in 1773 of his experiences, blames the competition of the opera, which paid its singers better : " Indeed all the *musici* in the churches at present are made up of the refuse of the opera-houses, and it is very rare to meet with a tolerable voice upon the establishment in any church throughout Italy. The *virtuosi* who sing here occasionally upon great festivals only are usually strangers, and paid by the time."

I have never made any comprehensive study of Christendom's service music, but have had casual experience of it in many countries, and my strong impression is that, grumble as we may at our own, ours is the best in the world, though followed (so far as standard of performance is concerned) at a short distance by that of the United States. I will even go so far as to say that it has never been my good fortune to hear really fine church music on the Continent. The Sunday afternoon before I wrote this I spent in Notre Dame at Paris. At his great west organ (nobler, by far, I should guess than any organ in the whole of Italy) our admired Dupré was pouring out his extemporizations, antiphonally to the chanting of a little choir of boys, standing before the altar and accompanied by the small chancel organ (sometimes played rather too loudly and with the too consistent use of the " Principal "). The voices were puny in volume, and the tone but poorish. And in any case is there artistic fitness in the contrast between a verse of plain-chant, diatonically accompanied by a few simple chords, and an extended interlude of blazing modern harmonies, with contrapuntal elaboration, and elaborate sequential pilings up or thinnings down, or a march-like staccato-chord passage, or a fugal exposition on a chromatic subject ? I dimly felt the incongruity of all this at Dupré's performance at the Albert Hall, but in the cathedral it forced itself violently upon me. I wish we could invite a congress of Continental church musicians to spend Holy Week with

Sir Richard Terry in Westminster Cathedral, and then (further to enlighten the Continent as to attainable standards of artistry and devotion in performance) send the Temple Choir for a long tour abroad.

Some Notes on the Foregoing

My publication of the foregoing essay, together with that of a plain-spoken criticism of a choir that visited London, under the title " The Vatican Choir," brought me a number of comments. Before saying what I much want to say about the importance of tone *qua* tone in musical performance, I propose to quote a few interesting passages from letters. A priest in Rome wrote to me :

You do not say what day you were in St. John Lateran, but from your remarks I judge it was Good Friday morning [*this is so*] and that what you heard was the Improperia or Reproaches. This, according to the enclosed programme, was by Casimiri himself.

I was present at the whole of the Easter Week service at St. John's, beginning on the Wednesday evening. The execution of the Responsoria at Tenebræ on that occasion was certainly very fine, as indeed it was on the evening following. But from Thursday on there was a notable deterioration which on Saturday morning ended in a complete rout. It struck me that there was more than carelessness there. I heard later that Mgr. Casimiri had kept his choir together with great difficulty during Holy Week.

The music you heard at the Gesu was executed by the ecclesiastical students of the German College (you may have remarked that their cassocks were red).

As a matter of fact, the ecclesiastical colleges have a
good reputation in music, notably the German and
the French. I have also heard the Irish and North
American students give a good account of themselves.

As to other points you raise, I have come to the
conclusion that, even supposing the Continental
boy's voice to be naturally inferior to that to which
we are accustomed in England and elsewhere, this
does not wholly account for the deficiency. Far
too little attention seems to be given to the production
and training of the voice both here and in France.

I had the good fortune to be present in the Sistine
at the Consecration of a Bishop by the late Pope
not long ago. One could not choose one's place
on such an occasion, and I found myself immediately
in front of the little cage, which you may remember
if you visited the Chapel when in Rome. Behind
this was the Sistine Choir, conducted by Mgr. Perosi
himself. The treble part was sung by *boys*, sustained
by two or three falsetto voices. I shall certainly
never forget the beauty of the Psalm, " Cantate
Domino . . . quia mirabilia fecit " (Perosi's own
composition) as rendered on that occasion. You
could not give a final judgment on Roman choirs
unless you had heard the Sistine.

About organs. Isn't the organ of St. Peter's also
part of the tradition you mention? See those pages
of Crawford's.

I well know the amazing pages on Church music in
Marion Crawford's " Ave Roma Immortalis." The
statement is there made : " The music sung in St.
Peter's, and, indeed, in most Roman churches, is never
rehearsed or practised. The music itself is largely in
manuscript, and is the property of the choirmaster,

or (as in the case of St. Peter's) of the Chapter, and
there is no copyright in it beyond this fact of actual
possession, protected by the simple plan of never
allowing any musician to have his part in his hands
except when he is actively performing it." (This was
written in 1898, and may no longer be entirely true.)

A letter from Christopher St. John said :

I gather you went only to St. Peter's and the
Lateran [this is not quite the case], where I agree
with you the music and the singing are the limit.
But had some one taken you to the Benedictine
Church of S. Anselmo on the Aventine you would,
I am sure, have been pleased with the monks' plain-
song. Their rhythm is wonderful (or was in 1912,
when I lived in Rome) ; and except at Quarr, the
headquarters of the Solesmes Benedictines, who first
restored the plain-song melodies and the method of
singing them to their original purity, I have never
heard finer devotional singing. There has been a
great improvement in the character of the music used
in Italian churches and in the method of singing since
Pius the Tenth's Motu Proprio counselling the use of
plain-chant, and the official music of the liturgy,
and the polyphonic music founded on it.

One or two letters received mentioned particular
churches in Italy where the singing is above the
average ; several spoke favourably of church music
in some places in Germany ; one or two confirmed
my poor opinion of the music at Notre Dame, Paris ;
one called attention to the admittedly admirable work
done by the Chanteurs de St. Gervais in Paris—" tons
of Palestrina, Vittoria, Allegri, Josquin, Schütz "

(" the headquarters of this body is 36, Boulevard de St. Germain, Paris, 6, and intending visitors to Paris can always get particulars of coming performances by writing there "), and two or three very warmly praised the choral music at the church that has been put at the disposal of the Russians in London—St. Philip's, Buckingham Palace Road. It is somewhat remarkable that amongst all my correspondence I did not have one contesting my general view that, on the whole, church music in this country is on a far higher level than church music abroad.

Now about this question of tone. I find one or two colleagues weakly disposed to condone the harsh tone of the so-called " Vatican Choir," which has once or twice visited this country, on the grounds that different countries have different tastes. I do not understand the argument. Is it maintained that all standards are purely relative, and that there is no such thing as good-tone-absolute ? Logically, this commits us to the doctrine that everything in art and life is to be judged strictly by " the custom of the country," and, for that matter, by the custom of the period. Here is a real lazy man's doctrine, and one which, if admitted, will stand as the eternal enemy of all progress. The morals of the Court of Charles II, the more sentimental side of Victorian art, French decoration of the Rococo period, everything from cannibalism to the Cockney accent, can be so justified, and the world shall ever more stand still. But, narrowing again to the special point, can anything be said for a method of voice production which renders impossible any tonal homogeneity, which gives you a delicate silver in *pianissimo* passages and a glaring scarlet in *mezzo-forte*, changing colour moment by moment like the fabled chameleon ? What unity of effect is possible when you break your vocal line into these small pieces, entrusting three words to a young cherub in the skies, and the following three to the newsboy from the next street ?

THE O.B. AND MUSIC

THEY don't sell Freia's apples in Covent Garden, and the fabled elixir of youth is understood to be replaced in the modern pharmacopœia by some highly expensive decoction of a monkey's thyroid gland. Pending the reduction in cost of this last commodity, there are certain temporary youth-extenders available. If feeling weary and old, put on to your gramophone the record of Bliss's " Rout " or turn to either of the volumes of reminiscences of Mr. Oscar Browning, of which the second has lately appeared (" Memories of Later Years "). The spirit of zest exhales from the old man as from the young one. I visited him in his Roman Palazzo not long since and found him, at eighty-five, just embarking upon a new and closer, critical and complete study of Byron's prose and poetry, and upon the founding of a little private society for the study of the whole of Mozart.

Every old Cambridge man knows The O.B.'s musical predilections. " First Mozart, then Bach, then Per-golesi " is the order of merit amongst composers, as he put it to me not long ago in a letter. " Pergolesi sends me wild. My Mozart concerts go splendidly every Monday at 5.30. We are now doing for the second time the six quartets dedicated to Haydn, and

the performers are very enthusiastic. Beethoven
has not a chance beside him!" But I do not think
The O.B. is a Beethoven-hater, like some others of
our young Mozart-wild musical men of to-day. He
was an interested attendant at the great Bonn
Festival of 1871.

George Grove was a very conspicuous figure as he
moved about with his finger in the newly published
volume of Thayer's "Life of Beethoven"; also
John Farmer, of Harrow, whose vocabulary of enthusiasm was more forcible than classical. When he said
that Beethoven made his soul sweat, Grove was much
disgusted.

A good deal of Beethoven's power of sweating our
souls has gone since then, for music yet more
emotionally calorific has become common. Yet the
passage probably hints at a quality we still recognize
in Beethoven, and one that is, I should guess, as little
attractive to the O.B. as Farmer's way of describing it
was to G.G. Beethoven is probably a little too dramatic for him. In fact, it comes again to this—Beethoven is not young enough to be a playmate for Oscar
Browning, for even in his most "unbuttoned" moods
Beethoven never forgets that he is of adult age. It
is Mozart's eternal youth that attracts The O.B., and
for a change from Mozart he will turn to Bach, who,
though he had his serious moods, remained essentially
young in spirit.

I do not know whether The O.B. has realized it,
but he is, in a sense, a living link with his adored
Mozart. For Mozart actually wrote music to the
order of The O.B.'s mother's dancing-master. Mozart,

in 1778, wrote the ballet music, " Les Petits Riens," for the great Noverre. Two years later Noverre retired on a royal pension, but eleven years after that the Revolution drove him to England, where he began professional life again, and gave dancing lessons to the girl who afterwards became The O.B.'s mother, choosing her to dance the minuet with him at the public exhibition of his pupils. Mr. Browning, as his books show, has himself in his day been a great dancer and a popular M.C. If at any time within the next twenty years, by the mercy of God and some refining of the hearts of men, the minuet should return to favour we shall look to him for a demonstration of the sound tradition.

When as a youth Sterndale Bennett went to Leipzig to be with Mendelssohn, " being under the impression (which was probably in general a correct one) that Handel was less familiar to the Germans than to the English, he asked Mendelssohn whether he knew a great deal of his music, and Mendelssohn snapped at him with the reply, ' Every note.' " Except that The O.B. cannot snap, that is probably the sort of reply you would get if you innocently asked him if he knew a good deal of Mozart. I remember his writing some Mozart articles for me in 1911, for a paper that I then edited, and pleading for the revival of the Flute and Harp Concerto, written by the composer as a young man, in Paris, for the Duc de Guines and his daughter. " It would be," he said, " a welcome addition to our concert-room programmes," but I have never yet heard it. He seems to have stumped a great Mozartean with that very work, for after celebrating New Year's

Day, 1916, with " a dish of buffalo, which I, in common with many Romans, had learnt to like," he continued the festivities the next day by attending the Augusteo concert, conducted by Sir Thomas Beecham, and further prolonged them by lunching with Sir Thomas at his hotel, a day or two later, and engaging in competition as to which of them knew Mozart best. " I beat him with Mozart's Concerto for flute and harp, which I knew better than he did, but when he played to me an air from ' Zaide ' which I had never heard, I confessed that he had won." Whether we shall ever see " Zaide " on our stage seems more than doubtful, but now that our great Mozart conductor has returned to the orchestral rostrum may we plead with him for a chance to make acquaintance with the much-praised concerto ? But the number of Mozart concertos few of us have heard must be large. All told, the concertos for various instruments number about fifty, and The O.B. has probably heard as many of them as any man living. There are, I believe, twenty-five for the piano alone, and Saint-Saëns played the lot :

When I was in London he played twenty-four, of which I heard sixteen. On one occasion he told us that the Concerto which he had just given he had played first as a boy of fifteen, being then over seventy. He therefore possessed all the right traditions. The only Mozart player I now care to listen to is Busoni, but then there is much of himself. The one hope of modern music is " Back to Mozart."

The last sentence indicates a certain attitude towards modern music on which, had I space, I should like to dwell a little. As it is I must content myself with but one further allusion to The O.B. as musician, this time as vocalist. There are records in these pages of his popular public performance of " The Baby on the Shore " ; he once saved his life from savages by giving them " Ta-ra-ra-boom-de-ay " ; in danger with Lloyd George and others in a launch off Gibraltar he calmed his companions by singing " Rule, Britannia ! " (of which he evidently knows not merely the chorus, but the first verse also—a rare accomplishment) ; and, driving to visit Newnham College with our present Queen, he joined her in " The Man that Broke the Bank at Monte Carlo " ! This last incident has since troubled him, since doubts have arisen as to Court etiquette on such an occasion.

NOTE.

Whilst this book was passing through the press came the regretted news of the death of Mr. Oscar Browning (at Rome, 6th October, 1923).

"RE YOUR LETTER TO HAND"

LET us turn for once from what the sober critic says to his readers to what his readers, much more amusingly, say to him. Some day, if no colleague steals a march on me, I shall write a book on this subject, but, as preface, I shall take the precaution of giving a copy of an affidavit, duly sworn before a Commissioner ; for there is to be remembered the Welsh reader who wrote to me, when I was discussing the Welsh musical taste :

Your quotations from supposed letters are scandalous ! Who can tell but that these are faked stuff ? As they stand one and all of us have the right to believe that you have manufactured them. This sort of thing is dishonourable, contemptible, and mean, and one's gorge rises at such a disgusting attitude. What evidence have we that you received letters from which you are supposed to cull ? Yes, what ?

I should like to regain the good opinion of Wales. Shall I do so by quoting to-day exclusively from English letters ? A word of caution for you in reading them, however. Every word quoted here actually appears in some letter received by myself—save that in every case names and places are changed. But do not try to identify the writers, or you will do somebody an injustice ; for there is not a single extract of which you are in the very least likely to guess the authorship correctly.

Firstly, I will take those businesslike correspondents who want their concerts or their relatives' concerts to be noticed. Usually they begin their letters with a tactful compliment, as, for instance, the Sussex lady who opens : " I know you have a kind heart beneath a rather grim exterior " (when did she see me ?) Then comes always some such request as this, from a fond mother :

My daughter asks me to forward you the enclosed programme and particulars of her concert at Sutton-on-the-Sands. Of course, you will understand that, naturally, she wishes any notice you may write to apply principally to herself and her pupils rather than to those names appearing in the second half of programme, some of whom are also professionals teaching in this neighbourhood.

Often with such letters as these are enclosed cuttings from the local Press. There is a long one before me, in which an opera performance was described by a provincial colleague of mine. He outlines the opera's plot in great detail, and praises every actor, but confines his serious musical criticism to this :

The chorus deserves praise, and its sympathetic rendering of " God Save the King " was cultured to a degree.

Another type of letter asks me to break out into spontaneous public congratulation as, for example,

the following, typed upon the headed business paper of
" James Linniker, Estate Agent, High Street, Wooding-
on-the-Wold, Lincs."

Hearty congratulations to Mr. and Mrs. Linniker,
of Wooding-on-the-Wold, on the occasion of their
golden wedding. Mr. Linniker has been organist
of the Wooding-on-the-Wold Parish Church for fifty-
three years.

Letters of this self-congratulatory character sometimes
come even from reputable publishing and concert-
giving firms, who, with the same consideration as is
shown by my correspondent, Mr. Linniker, save me
all possible trouble by setting out matter for my
columns exactly as it should appear in them. This
one is a few years old, and the firm to which it refers
no longer exists :

We have much pleasure in reporting the great
success that has attended the last series of concerts
given by the renowned publishing and piano-making
firm of Jenkinson, of Great Ormond Street, W. We
were especially charmed with the tone of the Jenkinson Piano used, and the new ballads published by
this firm and sung at these concerts should prove
very refreshing to vocalists throughout the country.
We understand that a further series will be given,
and we are confident that if the same high standard
is attained they will prove even more successful than
the first series. We would advise any of our readers
who have not yet been able to attend to do so at the
earliest opportunity.

In a few cases I have been asked to review music without seeing it, as, for instance, in the following from a foreign firm which sends me the review ready written and generously orders " copies of the issue of your journal in which the review appears, to the value of 10s."

Mr. Limburger's compositions are tone-pictures, delicate sketches. They are excellent for the cultivation of style and refined colouring, and the pupil will always play them with pleasure and decided gain, as they are an incentive to intelligent application.

It may be interesting to our readers to know that Mr. Limburger's sister is the remarkable painter in miniature who has executed portraits, by royal command, of the late King Vladimar of Ehrenbreitstein, the Grande Duchesse Amalie, the late Emperor and Empress of Russia, and many others—the beauty of Royalty and of the first families of several continents.

I could run on for some time with extracts from communications of that character, but prefer to turn to something more sympathetic—the communications from simple-minded, honest readers desiring musical guidance for themselves and their sons, daughters, nephews, nieces, and cousins. Many of these are in some way or other remarkable.

I have a son who is a Member of a Brass Band. He is also studying the Harmonium, Flute, Piccolo, English Concertina, etc., as well as Harmony and Counterpoint. Would you please advise him. . . .

No, madam, I would *not* ! Your son already knows a great deal more than I. Here follows a different type of letter, one with the ring of sincere repentance for wasted opportunities :

I am a little over twenty years old, and having studied the piano for three years with one of the best Manchester teachers, but I regret to say that I never practised anything like what I should have done. When Mother asked my teacher how I was getting on I believe he shook his head and said, If I would only practise, for I had the ability. I believe he tried every way to get me warmed to it. I often wish I had the same chance now. But, my dear sir, if you can help me in any way I shall be most delighted to try again. . . .

Alas ! What can the poor music critic do ? Who is he to restore to the aged penitent the years of her mis-spent youth ? Here is a letter I lately received ; though I read it with a real desire to help to settle the implied wager I had in the end to give it up :

I should be much obliged if you would express an opinion as to whom you consider the more classical composer, Wagner or Sullivan.

There all depends, of course, upon the writer's own understanding of the chameleon-word " classical."

Turning to the more distressing side of my corre-spondence, I quote a letter or two from stern moralists. Music critics are admittedly fierce creatures, but Critic critics are fiercer. (I fear that no " kind heart beats beneath *their* grim exterior ! ")

Dear Sir, If you are supposed to write musical criticisms, would it not be better to do so, instead of

merely furnishing us with paragraphs expressing your
personal prejudices ?

That may be called the pointed rapier ; here is the
heavy bludgeon :

Sir, Please " dry up " condemning and talking
such rot as *vulgar, commonplace,* etc., of works such
as . . . Who are you, and what have you done ?
Leave off and get and do something more useful for
a living.

SONNENBERG, SCHWYZ,
	July, 1923.